Developing Thinking Skills T' Creative Writing

Developing Thinking Skills Through Creati, ⌐. ⌐Ɫory Steps for 9–12 Year Olds is a practical and easy-to-use teacher resource helping children across a wide age and ability range to develop the skills necessary to write more effectively. Step-by-step instructions encourage children to tackle tasks of increasing difficulty while broadening their knowledge and experiences of fictional genres.

With chapters separated into distinct genres: ghost story, fantasy, science fiction, history, pirate story, thriller and Gothic horror, this book:

- Offers a summary at the start of each chapter to help teachers select the relevant activities.
- Covers multiple aspects of storytelling from narrative structure, plots, characters and settings to vocabulary, word choice, sentence structure and punctuation.
- Provides a cross referencing grid showing which aspects of writing appear in each chapter.
- Includes guidance notes, extension activities and general tips.

Adaptable to different teaching situations, this book offers the opportunity for teachers to work through the book genre by genre or take a 'skills route' with different activities from different chapters to create their own programme of study. Fully illustrated and supporting the requirements of the National Curriculum, *Developing Thinking Skills Through Creative Writing* is a valuable aid for all Key Stage 2 teachers.

Steve Bowkett is a former teacher and author of numerous books for teachers. He visits schools to run creative writing workshops for children and works as an educational consultant specialising in the areas of thinking skills and problem-solving, creativity and literacy.

Tony Hitchman has over 35 years of experience teaching throughout the primary age range in diverse schools, culminating in 11 years as a primary school Head Teacher. In his spare time(!), he has written scripts for the comic publisher DC Thomson, contributed cartoons and comic strips to various small press publications, illustrated educational books and collaborated with Steve Bowkett on *Using Comic Art to Improve Speaking, Reading and Writing* (2012).

Developing Thinking Skills Through Creative Writing

Story Steps for 9–12 Year Olds

**Steve Bowkett
and Tony Hitchman**

Routledge
Taylor & Francis Group

LONDON AND NEW YORK

First published 2020
by Routledge
2 Park Square, Milton Park, Abingdon, Oxon, OX14 4RN

and by Routledge
52 Vanderbilt Avenue, New York, NY 10017

Routledge is an imprint of the Taylor & Francis Group, an informa business

British Library Cataloguing-in-Publication Data
A catalogue record for this book is available from the British Library

Library of Congress Cataloging-in-Publication Data
A catalog record has been requested for this book

ISBN: 978-0-367-13994-0 (hbk)
ISBN: 978-0-367-13995-7 (pbk)
ISBN: 978-0-429-02959-2 (ebk)

Typeset in Helvetica
by Deanta Global Publishing Services, Chennai, India

Tony – To Sue – with thanks for all her love and support.
Steve – To Wendy, for patience and love.

Contents

Introduction

We intend this to be a practical resource book for helping children to learn more about writing short stories and to develop a raft of thinking skills as they do so. The very fact that you are reading this suggests that you think creative writing is at least enjoyable and, ideally, crucial in developing children's thinking and communication skills, their self-confidence and self-esteem. The writer and educationist Gail E. Tompkins (see readingrockets.org and https://www.jstor.org/stable/41405103 in the 'References and resources' section) lists seven reasons why teaching creative writing to children is important:

- To entertain.
- To foster artistic expression.
- To explore the functions and values of writing.
- To stimulate imagination.
- To clarify thinking.
- To search for identity.
- To learn to read and write.

We would add:

- To develop cognitive growth and organisational abilities.
- To increase one's ability to influence through language.
- To give structure and greater meaning to one's life.

This last point has a connection with Howard Gardner's theory of multiple intelligences (see for instance Rockett & Percival, 2002). Here, Gardner suggests that we possess a range of 'intelligences' that can evolve through time, i.e. that intelligence is not a single 'entity', nor is it fixed. In his earlier work Gardner identified 'linguistic intelligence', the potential to use and manipulate concepts using words. More recently, 'narrative intelligence' was added to the list (see the Mateus-Sengers website link in 'References'). It refers to the supposedly innate human ability to make sense of and learn from narrative structures, i.e. stories. One aspect of this idea is its practical value in helping one to live a fulfilling life, as we recognise that life, like stories, has a beginning, a middle and an end; chapters, settings, characters, conflicts, problems, journeys and resolutions. And from an early age, we know intuitively that good and bad exist in the world; that there will always be villains, and so we will always need heroes to restore harmony and balance. In this regard, Philip Pullman in his essay 'Imaginary Friends' (2017) asserts that by telling children fairy tales at an early age (and stories generally throughout childhood), coupled with the imaginative play that comes naturally to young children, they will develop a moral sense and grow up to be more fluent and confident not just with language but with any kind of intellectual activity, including the sciences. In addition to this, we feel that writing stories is an extension through childhood and beyond of the creative play we engaged in as youngsters, enhancing all of its established benefits.

Researcher of writing Donald H. Graves also makes the salient point that children (in fact all of us) have an inherent need to express ourselves (Graves, 1983). This can take many forms, although the advantage of expressing oneself through words is that skill and experience in writing have wide and practical applications in many areas of life. For a fuller exploration of and justification for teaching creative writing, see our chapter on 'General tips when teaching writing'.

Our approach has been to focus on a particular fictional genre in each chapter, offering a range of activities and techniques that help to develop the set of skills necessary to improve a child's writing and the thinking that underpins it. The chapters are broadly sequenced from simpler to more complex in terms of the activities themselves and the concepts that define and describe the different genres. Many of the activities within each chapter can be used in most of the genres we cover, however. We have tried to pick genres that children will enjoy, so you can either take the 'genre route' and encourage children to write a ghost story, a fantasy story, a science fiction story etc., or you can take the 'writing elements' route and cherry-pick particular activities from different genres to look at plotting, character, descriptive writing or whatever. Whichever route you take, the activities are underpinned by thinking skills, enhancing the how-to focus of the book.

To facilitate your use of this book, we've prepared a checklist showing which aspects of writing crop up in which chapters.

The book also contains:

- A summary of what's in each chapter so that you can see at a glance how the activities are sequenced.
- Some background information on each genre for your information and to share with your class as appropriate.
- Plenty of supporting images, including a range of visual planners that help children to interpret and represent information in different ways, thus boosting their visual literacy.
- Numerous cross-references between chapters so that you can see how writing elements and thinking skills apply across the range of genres.
- Thumbnail definitions of certain terms that are italicised through the book, which you might need to explain to the class.
- References and resources – books and websites referenced in the text that we've found useful and that complement and extend what we've set out to achieve.

Finally, as well as aiming to offer practical activities, we wanted to communicate something of the attitude and attributes required to evolve as a writer. These include determination, a willingness to learn and work hard, resilience in dealing with frustrations and setbacks but most of all an appreciation of the great pleasure and satisfaction to be found in turning thoughts and feelings into words on the page that other people can also enjoy.

Steve Bowkett and Tony Hitchman

1 Writing a ghost story

Summary of the chapter

- Introduction. Defining a ghost story. You can offer the children our definition and also ask them for their own ideas. Exploring the etymology of some common words found in ghost stories, such as 'ghost' and 'haunted'. What other relevant words can the children research using a dictionary and thesaurus?
- What does a good ghost story contain? Collect ideas from the class. Let the children use the list given as a reference to help them plan their own stories.
- First planning. Thinking of plot, characters, settings and objects. Any of these features can be used to generate ideas for the others. Questioning is the behaviour we want to encourage. So, asking about a magical book can create ideas about characters' motivations, which can lead on to thoughts about sequences of events. Example questions are given to show the children what's expected of them. What other questions can they think of?
- Research. Encourage children to read/watch/listen to some age-appropriate ghost stories. You may want to do this as a first step to introduce the genre and inform children's thinking to tackle the other activities in this chapter. Further research projects include exploring word origins, analysing ghost stories to see how other writers achieve their scary effects, discussing any ghost stories that the children have previously written, and discussing what scares readers in ghost stories and why.
- Story lines. This is a visual planning device. Once children understand the idea, they can use it to plot stories in other genres, plus pieces of nonfiction writing. We also aim to encourage the attitude that it's fine for children to change their minds as they plan, because it shows further thinking and decision-making skills.
- Characters. Here we introduce 'character templates' such as hero, villain and companion. We also look at character descriptions, plus touching on a few old-hat character situations that are best avoided.

– Settings. Encouragement for the children to think beyond the usual settings for a ghost story. We also point out that the reader's imagination fills in many of the details of a setting, so including just a few vivid descriptive details usually works better than writing long slabs of description.
– Atmosphere. Tips for creating atmosphere in a ghost story, plus advice for distinguishing between different emotions such as nervousness, fear and terror.
– Story starters 1 – plot suggestions.
– Story starters 2 – opening scenes.

Introduction

Ghost stories have been around for hundreds, if not thousands, of years and come from all over the world. They belong to the **genre** of **horror** fiction, which is part of the bigger category of **supernatural** fiction.

Ghost stories are usually meant to be scary, but they can also contain humour (such as the Scooby-Doo cartoons). Sometimes they are written or told to teach us something useful, acting as a kind of **parable** or **morality** tale. *A Christmas Carol* by Charles Dickens is a well-known example.

The word 'ghost' comes from an old form of English meaning 'spirit' or 'soul'. The word 'haunted' comes from an old version of French meaning 'to visit a place often', and may date back even further to the idea of 'to settle' or 'be home'. Ask the children how they think this earlier meaning fits in with what is found in some ghost stories.

What does a good ghost story contain?

A ghost, obviously. But an effective scary tale doesn't show the ghost too early. There might be signs of a ghost's presence before we ever see it.

For example, there could be –

● Unexplained draughts.
● Unusual voices or other sounds.
● 'Cold spots' – areas where the air chills you for no obvious reason.

- Doors opening or closing by themselves.
- Strange shadows and things glimpsed out of the corner of your eye.
- Objects that move by themselves or that you discover have been moved.
- Things that are not what they appear to be. For example, a face that turns out to be a pattern on wallpaper. Or a pattern on the wallpaper that turns out to be a face!
- A general atmosphere of tension or menace. For example, the sense that someone or something is watching you.
- Sudden surprises or shocks. For example, you open a door and a crow flies out of the room, just missing your face.
- A suitable location. We'll look at that when we come to settings on page 18.

Tip A general rule for writing good stories is 'less is more'. Advise the children not to overuse any of these features or others that they think up for themselves.

First planning

Planning a story beforehand will make writing it easier. A plan doesn't need to involve a lot of writing. The point of a plan is to get ideas into some sort of order. Discourage children from making up the story as they go along. Thinking time beforehand saves time later.

Remind the class that stories feature –

A plot.
Characters.
Setting or background.
Objects.

Tip A story can be planned by thinking about any of these. So, for example, if we choose an old book as one of the objects in a story and ask questions about it, we find that ideas for a plot come to mind as we think of some possible answers.

So, for example –

- Where did the book come from?
- How is it unusual?
- Why would a book have a lock on it?
- Where is the key?
- Why are one or more of our characters interested in it?
- How is it linked to the ghost (or ghosts) in our story?
- How can we use it to make our story a spooky one?

Think of at least one answer to each question before looking at our suggestions below.

Where did the book come from?

- Our main character bought it from a second-hand bookshop.
- It was left to the **protagonist** in a great uncle's will.
- Some kids found it in the woods.
- It appeared mysteriously on the doorstep one day.

How is it unusual?

- It is old and battered and filled with strange writing and drawings.
- After coming across it one or more characters start to have frightening dreams.
- Strange things now start to happen.
- The book begins to speak to one or more of the characters.

Why would a book have a lock on it?

- Because what's written in it is dangerous in the wrong hands.
- It is someone's private diary.
- The information inside is valuable.

Where is the key?

- On a chain around a character's neck (the villain?).
- Hidden close to where the book was found.
- It is lost forever, so you need a spell to open the book.

Why are one or more of our characters interested in the book?

- Because it allows their wishes to come true. (But why could this be a bad thing?)
- Because it is the diary of a ghost hunter and contains unsolved cases. (And what happened to the ghost hunter?)
- Because it contains maps of haunted places.
- Because our characters think it can lead to buried treasure.

How is it linked to the ghost or ghosts in our story?

- Some ideas above provide answers to the question.
- The book itself is haunted.
- The book contains information for raising ghosts or getting rid of them.
- It is a scrapbook of news clippings about a murder. The ghosts of the victims want **vengeance**!

How can we use it to make our story a spooky one?

- The book moves mysteriously from place to place.
- When characters handle the book, disturbing visions appear.
- People feel frightened when the book is nearby.
- A face or other scary things start to appear on the book's cover.
- When frightening **prophecies** are read aloud from the book, they soon come to pass.

> **Tip** Planning a story involves asking many questions, coming up with a few possible answers to each, then deciding which ideas best fit together. The more children can develop these skills, the easier planning and writing stories will become.

Research

Exploring and analysing stories to pick up tips on how to improve one's own writing begins to develop useful research skills such as observation, concentration, inference, speculation, reasoning and making judgements that will prove valuable throughout the children's schooling in many subject areas. Examples of kinds of research that children can do in planning a ghost story include –

- Read some ghost stories to see how other authors do it.
- Read about 'ghost sightings' where people say they have actually seen a ghost.
- Find some **synonyms** for the word 'ghost' to give the writing freshness and variety.
- Work with others in the class to **brainstorm** words that could be useful in the story – we'll look again at **vocabulary** below.

> **Tip** Reading or listening to ghost stories will probably give children more ideas to put into their own tales. It isn't wrong to use other people's ideas while they are learning to be better writers. In fact, **retelling** or **recounting** a story a child has enjoyed are useful skills to develop.

Story lines

One easy way to plan is to draw a straight line on a large sheet of paper representing the beginning, middle and end of a story.

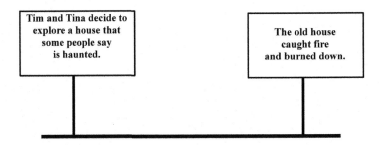

As the children think of their ideas, encourage them to write each one briefly on a sticky note and put it on the line where they think it will appear in the narrative. For example, the sticky note 'Tim and Tina decide to explore a house that people say is haunted' would go towards the left-hand side of the line, as this idea would be used near the start of the story. 'The old house caught fire and burned down' would go towards the right-hand side of the line if this scene comes near the end of the story.

Suggest that children don't need to set their stories in a spooky old house. The location might be a deserted funfair, a museum at night, dark woods, a ruined church with a graveyard or a locked multi-storey car park. Set the task of making a short list of other settings that could be suitable. Bear in mind that settings where the characters can't call for help create more tension in the story.

> **Tip** As a writer, it's fine to change your mind. Once children have placed their sticky notes they can be rearranged as the story plan develops. 'Strong' ideas can be placed above the line, while ones children aren't yet sure about (and may discard) can go below the line.

At this early stage of planning, ideas can be quite vague. For example, a child might like some 'danger' in the tale, or a 'chase' or a 'scary meeting'. General ideas like these can be written on separate sticky notes and placed where the child thinks those scenes might eventually appear.

> **Tip** Try to vary the peril. By its fifth appearance even the best ghost loses the power to shock. Similarly, chase after chase after chase can be tedious unless the location varies. So, as well as corridors, where else might there be a chase? Maybe battlements, woods, sewer tunnels or the moors in a storm, for instance. Also, think what opportunities each location has (rivers to ford, weapons to be found, places to hide).

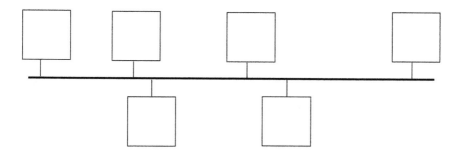

> **Another tip** Although a story has a beginning, a middle and end, children don't need to think about or write the start of the story first. Maybe there's a very exciting or scary scene in the middle of the story – it's fine to write that first. Once the story is planned, it becomes easier to write scenes in whatever order children choose.

Characters

Every story has **characters**. As a simple rule, there will be major characters and minor ones. Major characters usually include the **hero**, the **villain** and one or more **companions**.

The hero will have certain qualities in his or her character. These are sometimes called 'noble' qualities, ones that are good or that we can admire. These include courage, truthfulness, kindness and loyalty.

A 'hero' doesn't have to have any special powers or be really strong or a good fighter. Ordinary people can have heroic qualities. For example, imagine that a story features a group of children who are exploring a house that's supposed to be haunted. They hear frightening noises and start to run outside. Tim falls and twists an ankle. Tina, even though the scary noises are getting louder, goes back to help her friend. That counts as a heroic act. So, in any story two or more characters can be heroes, using the definition above.

Villains, on the other hand, have 'mean' qualities such as selfishness, greed, envy, dishonesty and ruthlessness. Villains can also be persuasive and appear to be kind and caring, when really they're out for their own ends.

Advise children not to make the villain simply evil or mad: there should be a reason for a villain's actions that the reader can accept. This might be revenge, a desire for power or a sense of entitlement.

Tip Heroes are more believable if they aren't perfect but have a flaw or a weakness of some kind. Also, in some stories heroic qualities might not show themselves in a character until that person is tested. For instance, Tina might have thought she was a coward until she bravely went back into the old house to help Tim.

Similarly, the most believable villains have at least one quality that we can like, or at least understand. For instance, a character that is evil might show great kindness towards animals.

Companions are useful in stories because they give more opportunities for writers to use dialogue and can be listeners/questioners when the main characters are explaining something. Also, if children are writing in the **third person**, the characters can split up and so the narrative switches between them as the story goes on.

Encourage children not to make a companion just like the hero, but to give him or her a different personality. Maybe a companion could be more cautious, more reckless and more superstitious or have a skill the hero doesn't have, like being a computer whiz or being able to solve puzzles.

Tip Do not have characters splitting up to investigate, say, a haunted house. That's a really old and worn-out idea. Also, do you really think any sensible person would explore a scary place alone? Having said that, it's OK for characters to become separated somehow by accident or by some other device such as a hidden trapdoor or being deliberately separated by the villain. This creates drama and tension.

Activities

acceptance	detachment	hilarity	regret
affection	determination	hope	relief
aggravation	disappointment	hopelessness	remorse
agitation	disapproval	horror	repentant
aloofness	discomfort	hostility	resentment
ambition	discouragement	humiliation	resignation
amusement	disgust	humility	respect
anger	dismay	indifference	responsibility
annoyance	distress	impatience	restlessness
anticipation	dread	impetuosity	revulsion
anxiety	eagerness	impulsiveness	sadness
apathy	ebullience	inadequacy	safety
appreciative	ecstasy	incredulity	satisfaction
apprehension	effusiveness	inferiority	security
assurance	elation	innocence	sentimentality
attraction	embarrassment	inspiration	serenity
awe	empathy	interest	seriousness
awkwardness	empowerment	irascibility	shame
bitterness	enchantment	irritation	shock
bliss	encouragement	jealousy	smugness
boredom	enjoyment	joy	sombreness
camaraderie	enthusiasm	lethargy	sorrow
capability	envy	listlessness	startlement
caution	esteem	loneliness	stubbornness
chagrin	excitement	love	superiority
cheer	exhilaration	melancholy	suspicion
comfort	exuberance	misery	sympathy
compassion	fascination	nervousness	tenacity
composure	fear	nostalgia	tenderness
concern	flippancy	optimism	tension
confusion	fondness	outrage	terror
contempt	forgiveness	passion	thrill
contentment	friendliness	pathos	unease
coolness	frustration	patience	uncertainty
courage	fulfilment	peacefulness	vitality
curiosity	fury	pessimism	warmth
cynicism	gentleness	petulance	wistfulness
dejection	gladness	pity	wonderment
delight	gratification	pleasure	
depression	greed	power	
desire	grief	powerlessness	
desolation	guilt	pride	
despair	happiness	rage	
despondency	helplessness	reassurance	

From this list of abstract nouns (all of which are the names of emotions) please try the following –

- Ask pairs or small groups of children to pick a few words they don't understand and find out their meanings.

- Pick a few emotions and research several synonyms and an antonym.
- Select up to ten emotions that characters might experience during a ghost story. As an optional extra, grade the emotions from mild to intense.
- Create a template of four columns with at least ten rows. Label the columns as below. For each emotion you'd find in a ghost story, create a sentence turning the abstract noun into an adjective and then a verb (modifying the word as necessary). In the right-hand column, think of a situation where that emotion would be experienced.

Name of emotion	Adjective	Verb	Situation
Excitement	This was a very exciting adventure.	Billy was excited and scared at the same time.	Going on the Ghost Train at the funfair.
Fear	They saw a fearful sight.	The children feared the darkness.	Exploring a spooky old house.
Loneliness	Katya spent a lonely night, unable to sleep.	(no verb)	Camping out alone in the woods.

When writing a short story, descriptions of characters need to be brief but able to allow readers to picture people in their mind's eye. Also, there is no need to have all the descriptive details in one place. So, the reader might be told that a female character is ten years old, tall, with fair hair, but mention later that she is shy, or really clever or whatever.

Tip Character details are also revealed through **dialogue**. So somewhere in the story Tim might say to Tina, 'Wow you worked that out quickly. You're really clever!'

Activity

Here are a few character descriptions.

- In the first one, decide which details to leave out or put elsewhere in the story.
- In the second one, think of a few details that could be added.
- For the third one, write a short dialogue between this character and one or two others where we learn something about what at least one of the characters looks like, or something about their personality.

    1. Tina is 10 years old. She is tall and has fair hair, which she likes to wear in a ponytail. Her favourite hair elastic is green with silver glitter on it. Tina has always been a bit of a tomboy (though she doesn't tell anyone about the doll her older sister bought her last Christmas, which she cuddles each night to get to sleep). Tina doesn't like wearing dresses and enjoys sports. Her all-time favourite food is chicken curry. She enjoys reading and is top of the class at science.

    2. Tim is 11. He has black hair. He likes computers. He is quite a fast runner.

    3. Dimpul is almost 12 and is tall for her age. She was born in Goa in India but came to live in this country when she was 5. She has an open, friendly personality and she enjoys meeting new people. Her friends all agree that she has a kind-looking face and that she is nearly always smiling. She likes to wear colourful clothes and jewellery, especially beaded necklaces, bracelets and earrings that she makes herself.

Tip Get the most out of the ideas. Looking again at the description of Tina –

- The fact she is a tomboy might lead to her friends daring her to go into an old house (or wherever) by herself.
- She has a favourite hair elastic. Maybe she is in a dangerous situation and drops it where she hopes her friends will find it and recognise it.
- Perhaps her knowledge of science proves useful in the story.

Another tip Once children have created some characters, they can be used in other stories. That will save time, but also the writer will get to know them better.

Activity

Write a short description of this character. From the way he looks, what sort of person do you think he is? What can you guess or infer about his background? If you featured him in a ghost story, what role might he play and why?

Activity

Here is a group of characters. Think about the different roles characters can play in stories. For example; hero, villain, companion, follower, teacher, logical thinker, emotional person, victim, **stooge** etc. Add to the list and give a label to each of the characters in the group.

Activity

Imagine that you were featuring a mysterious mirror in your ghost story. Each of these characters looks into the glass. Describe their reactions and, from those reactions, what do you think each of them sees reflected?

Settings

Choosing the setting of a story is an important decision that must be made early in the planning. It's easy to grab at the old favourites such as a spooky castle (on a stormy night), an old house or a graveyard. There's nothing wrong with that, but ask children also to consider other locations that don't usually appear in such tales. Thinking about a busy shopping mall, a quiet country village, a circus, a train or bus, a supermarket, a school etc. throws up new ideas for a plot.

Activity

Advise that settings are usually more believable for a reader if they are places that the writers know themselves. When you describe a location, include a few vivid details rather than paragraph after paragraph of description. Remember that the reader's imagination will fill in a lot of the features of the setting anyway. To prove this, let's use the idea of a circus. Simply reading that word, did you notice how your mind created a rich and detailed picture of the sights, sounds and perhaps smells of a circus? And maybe remembered feelings of excitement too, and perhaps nervousness watching some of those fast rides?

Here are some suggestions for the setting of a ghost story. Choose one or more to use in your own writing. Or, use dice rolls to choose two locations at random. The first is where your story begins and the second is where your story ends. What happens in between?

Locked up funfair	Country lane	Seashore	Ancient mansion	Canal towpath	Old railway line
Night bus / train	Deserted warehouse	Stone circle	Museum at night	Remote hills	Ordinary house
Boarded up flats	Old castle	Strange village	Library	Shopping mall	Woodland path
A park	Abandoned church	Graveyard	River	Foggy street	Waste ground
Tumbledown house	Old fashioned hotel	Allotments	Alley	Accident blackspot	Junkyard
Empty school	Industrial estate	Overgrown garden	Lonely road	Lake	Haunted inn

Activity

Here are some visual examples of settings. Choose one and write two short descriptions of the place. Make the first one 'ordinary' and non-frightening, but make your second description as eerie and scary as you can.

Atmosphere

In a story, atmosphere means the mood or feeling the writer wants to create, so that the reader can feel something of what the characters are feeling. Atmosphere is evoked by –

- Description of places and things.
- Description of the characters' body language, reactions and facial expressions.
- What the characters say to each other.
- What different characters are thinking.

In a ghost story, the characters are probably feeling nervous, uneasy, frightened or even terrified.

Tip Instead of just saying, 'The storm made Steve feel frightened', add some details about the storm and what it *feels* like to be frightened. So maybe, 'The wind gusted and made the windows in the old house rattle. Steve felt frightened. His heart was racing and his fists were clenched as he glanced nervously at the deep shadows in the room'.

Activity

Nervous, uneasy, frightened and terrified are really describing different feelings. That is to say, the words are not exact *synonyms*. It's best if you write from your own experience, but that's not always possible. Most of us have probably felt uneasy, nervous and frightened at times and possibly even terrified (though this is a rare emotion for many).

So, if you have felt nervous in the past, consider –

- What did your body feel like at that point (e.g. heart beating faster, muscles tense and palms sweating, maybe)?
- Do you think nervousness feels the same in different situations? So, if you were nervous just before taking a test, does that feel the same as being nervous, say, walking along a deserted street at night? (Some of you may

think yes and some no. If yes, are there any common features in those situations? If no, what are the differences in your feelings?)
- Look at the list headed: 'What does a good ghost story contain?' on page 5. Pick a few of the examples, decide on the emotion you want your characters to feel and write a short scene to try and get your reader to appreciate those emotions. Do this before reading the example below.

Here is the thinking we did before we wrote the scene –

- Details – Unusual voices or other sounds. Things that are not what they appear to be. For example, a face that turns out to be a pattern on wallpaper. A general atmosphere of tension or menace; for example, the sense that someone or something is watching you.
- Characters – Three friends: Sarah, Nabila and Robert.
- Setting – An empty council house on an estate that is going to be redeveloped. Many of the houses are boarded up. Front and back gardens are overgrown. There is no one about on the streets. It is a cold, grey autumn day in the late afternoon.
- Atmosphere – Unease that turns into fear.

Nabila still thought that this was a stupid idea, but of course Robert wanted to prove that boys were braver than girls. And Sarah would do just about anything that her big brother told her to do.

The three of them were standing in the back garden of an empty house on Nelson Road, a street of abandoned houses waiting for the developers to move in. The garden was a mass of overgrown grass, nettles and untidy lilac bushes whose branches thrashed about in the cold October wind. The sky was overcast and there was fine rain in the air.

'So', Nabila said almost angrily, 'are you going in first, Big Man?'

Robert looked again at the open back door swinging in the wind and strained to see to the end of the shadowed passageway.

'Um, yeah. That's why we came. Follow me – if you've got the guts'.

He stepped inside with the girls a pace behind.

If anything, it felt even colder in the dingy passageway than outside. The air had a still, dead quality to it as if it had not been disturbed for a long time – as though no one had *dared* to disturb it for a long time. Nabila shivered, because of the chill perhaps. She did not want to admit that she was already getting scared.

They passed the gutted shell of a kitchen. The walls were streaked with black patches of mould and there were mouse droppings scattered about the tiled floor. The air smelt musty. Nabila wrinkled her nose. 'This is an unwholesome place', she thought. 'A sad and lonely and forgotten place'. She remembered Robert saying someone had told him that the house was haunted. Already her imagination was conjuring up ghosts with distorted faces looming out of the shadows – she made an effort to put such thoughts aside.

The children moved on, reaching the end of the passageway. A flight of stairs rose into the semi-darkness of the first floor. The stair carpet was rotten with damp. To the left, the door to the front room stood open. The room itself was a silent, empty space. Cobwebs and strings of dust, wafting softly in a gentle draft, hung from the bare bulb in the ceiling. Robert tried the light switch.

'Might have realised the power would be off', he muttered.

'The daylight is going', Nabila said, her voice trembling slightly. 'And you didn't bring a torch'.

'Yeah, well'. Robert had nothing more to say. By the tone of his voice, Nabila thought that maybe he was regretting his earlier bravado.

They stood there, filled with indecision.

By the fading light, Nabila cast her gaze across the grime-streaked walls of the front room. The paper, hanging off in strips, had an ugly floral pattern that, because of the way the shadows fell across it, resembled a twisted, monstrous face. And perhaps because of a crack in the window glass, a gentle draught was stirring the yellowed net curtains, making them look like ghostly veils.

'I'm frightened', Sarah admitted. Robert made an impatient tutting noise, proving to Nabila that he was getting edgy too.

'I think we should –' she started to say, when they all heard quick footsteps pattering across the bare-boarded floor of the room directly above. And then they heard someone giggling, almost hysterically – a woman's voice, followed by a rushing sound like waves swirling up on a distant shore.

Sarah let out a thin scream of fear and clung to her brother.

Points to note –

- The scene is written in the third person, but from Nabila's point of view. Usually, if you want to change the viewpoint to another character, you should begin a new scene.
- Notice how we have put in details of sights, sounds and smells to make the descriptions more vivid.

- We tried to develop the characters' relationships even though the scene was short, by Robert showing off how brave he was, Nabila's disapproval of what they were doing and Sarah's loyalty to her big brother. Trying to create believable characters – 'real' people – helps the reader to identify with their fear.
- Ghost stories work better if ghosts are not shown too early. By describing sounds from the floor above, but not describing the ghost itself (if it is a ghost!), we aimed to get the reader's imagination to do more of the work.

How could the scene be improved, do you think? Would you have written it differently?

Think about your answers before reading on…

- The characters were not described physically, other than to say they were children and that Sarah was younger than Robert. How did you imagine them? What details from your own imagination would you add to improve the scene?
- How would the scene have been different written from Sarah's point of view, or Robert's? Pick one of those characters and try rewriting it from their point of view and using your own ideas.
- When we were planning the scene, we presumed that the house was actually haunted. But what if it wasn't? What non-ghostly explanations can you think of for the running footsteps, the woman's giggle and the rushing sound?

Story starters 1 – Plot ideas

Here are some suggestions for building a ghost story. Encourage children to change them or combine them if they want to –

1. The phantom of a grey lady appears at the same time every year in a tumbledown mansion. A group of investigators tries to find out why.
2. A gang of jewel thieves hides in a house that is rumoured to be haunted. They create various sounds and lights to strengthen the rumour, hoping to keep people away.
3. Two ghosts that were friends in life wander around a town. If they perform three good deeds, they can move on. They can allow people to see them, and they can change the way they look, but they cannot directly affect the physical world.

4.   A group of children witness the ghostly vision of a car crash, but when they investigate they find that no such accident ever happened at that spot. They try to find an explanation for what they have seen.

5.   Some children find an object (choose what) that can summon ghosts. How do they use it?

6.   The ghost of a murdered person seeks justice. Tell this story from the ghost's point of view.

7.   A ghostly hand drags Eleanor's best friend Annie into a second-hand wardrobe that Annie's parents have bought. When Eleanor looks inside, her friend has vanished. How can she rescue Annie? (Use male characters, or a mixture of male and female, if you like.)

8.   A ghost seeking justice leaves clues that a group of friends can follow to find his or her killer.

9.   Some children coming home from shopping in town catch a late bus home. But the bus is not what it seems…

10. Our main character starts to receive phone calls from a millionaire who has died, revealing where they have hidden their most recent will.

Story starters 2 – Opening paragraphs

1.   You could smell the apples, sweet and tempting, in the still September air. We were crouched down behind clumps of willow herb overlooking the allotments. The purply-pink flowers had withered and died, and by Christmas the patch would be nothing more than dried sticks, giving no cover at all. But for now, we were camouflaged, hidden from everyone except a small terrier who came and sniffed at us before Brian scooted him on his way.

2.   Shadowfane Manor is a large Elizabethan house that has gone to ruin now. It lies almost forgotten within dense oak woods in a corner of rural England. No one thinks of going there, especially the local people who regard the place with dread, although they can never be persuaded to say why.

3.   'I hate it! I hate it! I hate it!' I yelled, letting the anger feelings grow and grow until I was in one of my huge red rages. When I got like that, Ben and Jess just stayed out of my way and Mum and Dad would do just about anything to calm me down. Not that they could do much right now though, because nowhere was open on Christmas Day. I gave my rocking horse a petulant kick and scooped up its wrapping paper and started tearing it

into shreds. I knew that underneath the temper there was disappointment and jealousy. I'd got a stupid rocking horse and Ben had got a smart new bike and Jess a new smartphone. Did my parents think I was still a kid or what!

4. Barchester Mansion wasn't really a mansion of course. We just said that because it was *scarier* when we walked past at night. Actually, it was the last house on the street – number 42 Auriga Road – just on the edge of the park. And in the darkness, when we were coming home from play, we'd stand in the shadows and talk about the dead thing that lived there, the thing that had once been Old Man Barchester.

5. I was sitting beside my Dad as we drove home from the cinema. It was quite late, after eight o'clock, and because of the lashing rain we'd be getting home after my usual bedtime. As we turned a corner, the car's headlights picked out a lone figure standing on the verge. I think it was a girl, about my age, because although she had a hood pulled up over her head I could see her long fair hair matted to her face with the wet. 'She looks ever so cold and miserable Dad', I said. 'Shall we offer her a lift?'

6. Powell grinned fiercely as the ancient sandstone crumbled away beneath his pickaxe, revealing the untouched seal beneath. 'We found it', he whispered, as though talking to himself. 'At last we found it – the legendary Kay-Toh-Bah Diamond'. Davies was hardly in the mood to argue. What they had found was an intact seal. It might be another of the many false leads they had come across during their search. Or maybe the tomb beyond (if it was a tomb) had been looted ages ago by thieves that entered by some other route. And even if the lost and priceless jewel of the Tyrant Queen Quaraya was to be found inside the hill, who could say what dangers lay ahead for the two men standing there sweating under the fierce Egyptian sun?

7. By a gleam of pale moonlight, Eleanor saw the shadows moving towards her. They came snaking, sneaking, curling, crawling out from among the trees like the great unfolding of a wizard's black robes. They swept across the open space and left a swathe of dead grass behind. They swooped up to treetop height then sank low as a slave's bowed back. They twirled around and within and among themselves and became an old woman's tatters, slung about bony shoulders.

8. 'Come on, you ghosts, come and get me!' His voice, all puffed out with bravery, echoed over the grass until it was lost in the noise of the wind booming above the ridge. He heard his friends giggling behind him but

stayed where he was, ten steps out in the darkness, arms opened wide, his eyes closed, his face tilted upward to the moonlit sky. None of the others had dared to do this; not one of them would scramble out of the warm cosy bubble of their tent and dare the ghosts to appear.

9.   I tried to stop him before he drove off, but I was too late. As he pulled away across the tarmac towards the front gates, I saw through his rear window that the back of the car was filled with swirling shadows. And I was sure that I could hear, above the grumble of the engine, a long, high, piping scream.

10.   We came from the alley into a street I didn't recognise. There was no one around, no cars parked outside houses and none going by. Heavy curtains were pulled across every window. It was a weird stillness, made worse somehow by the thin mist that curled very slowly in the air, like veils. 'This isn't our street', I said. 'In fact, it's not even our town'. Somehow I knew we had come through to another place, somewhere cold and gloomy and, for some reason, frightening.

2 Writing a fantasy story

Summary of the chapter

- Introduction. Defining fantasy as a genre, which includes many sub-genres. Touching on the idea of motifs and conventions in genre fiction. An important point to make to pupils is that while, by their nature, fantasy stories are 'fantastical', they can still explore important real-life themes such as good versus evil, different moral dilemmas and the role and qualities of the hero figure. Also point out that even in fantasy, the story has to be believable, insofar as the plot must be internally consistent and things must happen for good reasons. This applies also, and perhaps especially, to the use of magic in fantasy stories. Apart from that, it's often the case that using magic comes at a price.
- Themes are the bedrock on which stories are built. Activities include looking at common themes in fiction and in the news. Pupils may also choose themes from a list. Invite the class to think about how themes can reflect people's values and beliefs and what they regard as important in their lives.
- Narrative elements and a template for 'quest' stories. Help to familiarise children with the basic building blocks of most stories: hero, villain, journey, partner etc. A narrative template is also offered that can act as a visual planning tool. This works especially well for fantasy stories but can be applied to other genres.
- Motifs. Defining motifs (or tropes). Using a grid of motifs (that can be applied to any genre) as a way of adding detail to an evolving storyline. Follow on by asking pupils to list motifs – people, creatures, locations, objects and abstract ideas – that are specific to fantasy stories. Here is an opportunity to introduce or reinforce the notion of cliché and how to modify clichés to freshen up a plot.
- Settings. Using a 6x6 grid allowing pupils to mix-and-match locations for a fantasy story either by deliberately choosing or selecting randomly using dice rolls.

- Story threads. These are features of a plot that are woven together into a story. Highlight the deliberate vagueness of the language. This allows room for various interpretations and use in different genres. Encourage children to refer to the list when planning their stories. A further activity is to ask children to identify story threads in other narrative forms such as books, films and comics.
- Cliché in fantasy. Encouraging pupils to consider various possibilities for characters, settings objects etc. rather than snatching at the first thought.
- Design a... character, costume, creature, weapon. Some visual examples are given. Children can combine or otherwise modify the suggestions to create their own. Here is a further opportunity to revisit cliché and stereotyping.
- Story starters 1 and 2. A selection of plot ideas and opening scenes.

Introduction

The word 'fantasy' derives from the Greek meaning 'imagination, appearance' and has connections with 'phantom', from *phantazein*: 'make visible'. It is a rich and complex genre that has a number of **subgenres**. One website currently lists 58! Other sources include science fiction under the fantasy umbrella, though we would argue that SF is a genre in its own right. Having said that, genres can and do overlap, so that there are indeed stories that include aspects of SF and fantasy, horror and fantasy, SF and horror and so on. As with learning to write within any genre, becoming familiar with the motifs and conventions of that kind of fiction is important –

- Motif – a constituent feature within a story that helps to define and describe a genre. A motif can be a character, an object, a creature, a setting, even a statement/clip of dialogue etc.
- Convention – those things that you would conventionally expect to find in a story of a given genre. So, a dragon, for example, is a motif conventionally found in fantasy stories.

As children become more familiar with the motifs and conventions of different genres, they will feel increasingly confident in using them *un*conventionally, i.e. in a more original way. An extension of this is a willingness to explore those less-visited areas where genres overlap – see for example the note on Gothic fantasy below.

Exploring subgenres is beyond the scope of this book, though we would like to highlight a few important distinctions –

- High fantasy. This usually involves a hero on a quest through magical realms. It is also known as sword and sorcery.
- 'Everyday fantasy' or 'low fantasy'. Here, the fantasy emerges out of the ordinary day-to-day world and forms a backdrop to people's mundane lives ('mundane' here meaning the earthly world, rather than being something dull or monotonous). We fondly remember the books of writer Alan Garner, who is a master of this kind of fantasy (see 'References and resources').
- Gothic fantasy, also called Gothic horror or simply Gothic fiction. Older children might enjoy exploring this subgenre, where aspects of fantasy are mixed with darker and more frightening elements of horror. The atmosphere of such stories is usually gloomy and filled with a sense of dread.

When writing fantasy (or indeed any kind of story), children must bear in mind that the characters' motivations and the situations they find themselves in must be believable within the context of the narrative. Just because a story is labelled fantasy doesn't mean that 'anything goes'. The plot must be logically consistent, and things must happen for reasons that make sense. As an example, the writer Douglas Hill once woke with a vision of a waterfall that was cascading upwards into the sky. He imagined the hero of the novel cresting a hill and coming upon the thunderous roar of the water tumbling into the heavens. 'But I won't use it', Doug said, 'because it's just a pretty picture and doesn't make sense in the story'. (Personal communication)

Themes

A theme is the central idea on which a story is built. The most basic theme is 'good versus evil', which naturally leads to the idea of a hero fighting for good and righting wrongs and a villain creating problems and mayhem for evil and selfish ends.

Activity

One good 'off the shelf' source for themes is proverbs. These will convey the concept of a theme to the children and may also give them ideas for stories. Examples include –

- A fool and his money are soon parted.
- A friend in need is a friend indeed.
- A short cut is often a wrong cut.
- All that glistens is not gold.
- As you sow, so shall you reap.
- Enough is better than too much.
- Hope is the last thing that we lose.
- Knowledge is power.
- Oaks fall when reeds stand.
- Rumour is a great traveller.
- There is no true love without jealousy.
- You can't teach an old dog new tricks.

> **Tip** Encourage children not simply to accept these ideas as 'received wisdom'. Can they think of situations where the advice of a proverb does not apply? Can they find pairs of proverbs that are contradictory?

Ask what 'seed stories' (a story idea in one or two sentences) come to mind as you present them with a proverb. For example –

- As you sow, so shall you reap. A man comes upon a book of spells and uses them to become richer and more powerful, but he has not thought about the consequences.
- Oaks fall when reeds stand. An enemy invades the country of a mighty king. The king is determined to confront the invaders with an equally powerful army of his own. His daughter, however, warns that this is a dangerous move and suggests a better way to win…
- An evil wizard spreads rumours about a king who once imprisoned him, hoping to cause a revolt in the country.

Another way of helping children to begin developing a plot around a proverb is to use the 'once upon a time technique', so –

> Once upon a time there was a rich man who was rather foolish and rather greedy. One day a wayfarer knocked on his door and begged for some water. He had been travelling for many days and was tired, hungry and thirsty. Little did the rich man know that the wayfarer was also a trickster and a liar. Noticing the precious items in the rich man's home, the trickster said that he was on a journey to find a magic sword. It was rumoured to be owned by a knight who lived in the Farlands and who had fallen on hard times. 'If only I could raise enough money', said the wayfarer, 'I could buy the sword from this desperate knight and by its magic increase my wealth and power many times...'

This is a more sophisticated technique, as it asks children to 'compose' narrative in a stream-of-consciousness way rather than just have the basic idea for a plot. Even so, as children become more confident in relying on their imaginations, many of them find that they can readily make up storylines as they go along.

Other themes to be found in fantasy stories include –

- Ambition and its consequences.
- Loyalty.
- Betrayal.
- Courage.
- The underdog battles through/resilience.
- Sacrifice.
- Deception.
- Jealousy.
- Coming of age/initiation into adulthood.
- War (between good and evil, good and good and evil and evil).
- Survival against the odds.
- Prophecies and all the issues they raise.
- Fate versus free will.
- The 'chosen one' in all its many manifestations.
- Mastering (or failing to master) the darkness within.
- The end of an age or era.
- Exploring the forbidden and the consequences that follow.

- An event that gives power to or transforms a character.
- Powerful creatures that have a hidden weakness.
- Dreams that come true.

We see then that while some themes suit themselves more to fantasy or science fiction, as a rule they work at a deeper level than genre – 'survival against the odds', for example, could be interpreted in a number of ways and explored in stories of any genre.

Tip Looking at the Motifs Grid (page 39) and the list of story threads (page 43) in conjunction with a chosen theme or themes will help children to build a storyline.

The counter flip game

Themes tend to be broad and abstract ideas. To help children explore them, you can try the counter flip game. Here, children simply ask yes/no questions around a chosen theme (and in this case within the fantasy genre), flipping a two-colour counter or a coin to get an answer. So, taking as an example: 'An event that gives power to or transforms a character or characters', questions that children might ask include –

- Does the event happen to one person?
- Does it happen to the hero?
- Does the event involve magic?
- Is the person transformed physically?

Both yes and no answers are useful. A yes answer supplies a piece of information that can be incorporated into the evolving storyline and that may form the basis for a further question. A no answer means that children have to use their imaginations to come up with other possibilities. An example of such a 'question chain' is –

- Does the event happen to the hero? No.
- Does the event happen to the villain? No.

- Does the event happen to the hero's sidekick? No
- Does the event happen to someone the villain knows? No.

Sometimes when a string of no replies happens, children can feel they are 'painting themselves into a corner', though with a little ingenuity a way forward can be found –

- Does the event happen to a minor character who goes on to become the hero/villain?
- Does the event happen to a creature?
- Does someone say the event will happen, when in fact it doesn't?

Once a yes answer is given, children can begin asking about the nature of the event or come up with questions to discover what the characters look like and what their histories are.

> **Tip** Sometimes, and increasingly when they use this technique, children know their own minds – they know what they want the answer to be. In that case, advise them not to gamble with the answer by flipping the counter but simply to decide for themselves what they want.

Narrative elements

These can be considered as the building blocks of a story, the supporting structure where themes are the foundations. Once children understand the function of these narrative elements, they can apply them across all genres and use them analytically when reading other people's stories.

Hero – embodies the 'noble' qualities of the human being, including courage, self-sacrifice, generosity, kindness, compassion and selflessness. The hero need not be physically strong and tends to be more interesting if he or she has weaknesses or flaws. The function of the hero is to resolve the problem the villain has created and restore balance and harmony to the world.

Villain – represents the mean and selfish qualities of the human being. Although sometimes simply misguided, the villain's motives are usually selfish

and evil and often involve acquiring more personal power and wealth, sometimes combined with a revenge motive against the hero and others. See the
Figure on page 37 for further traits of villainous characters.

Problem – a story's central problem is created by the villain in his or her quest
for personal gain and often leads to secondary problems and crises that, in narrative terms, enrich the plot.

Journey – resolving a problem sends the hero on a journey (the quest motif),
which involves physical travel to encounter challenging situations but is also a
transformative experience: often the hero is tested to the limits and discovers
new depths of courage and resilience.

Partner – most usefully, the partner is a major character linked with the hero,
villain or both. The partner opens up the opportunity for dialogue and subplot,
and when attached to the hero can serve to highlight his or her weaknesses
and failings as well as strengths and achievements.

Help – help can arrive in several forms; as other characters, as happen-
stance (but don't overuse coincidence) and in fantasy stories as supernatural
intervention by the gods or other creatures. Putting the hero in a situation where
help is needed humanises that character for the reader.

Knowledge and power – means the gaining and losing of the advantage
between the major players through the story. Such advantage can take many
forms (see the motifs grid on page 39 and the list of story threads on page 42).
Building this element into a story maintains tension and excitement and leads
to a richer narrative.

Object – commonly the story's central problem occurs because of the villain's desire to get hold of an important, powerful and dangerous object. The
hero's job is to retrieve the object, either by finding it first or taking it from the
villain, then return it to its rightful owner or place. Sometimes the object is in
fragments that need to be gathered up, and sometimes the object is such a
potential threat that it needs to be destroyed.

Traits of the villain

Ambitious– willing to do anything to succeed	**Unforgiving** – intolerant of people's mistakes	**Opinionated** – won't accept other views/arguments	**Dishonest** – readily cheats and misleads to achieve aims	**Charismatic** – inspires devotion in others	**Possessive** – will cling to possessions, followers etc
Persuasive – can bend others to his/ her will	**Superior** – believes he/she is better than others	**Greedy** – always want more – power, wealth etc	**Violent** – readily uses physical force to damage or kill	**Skilled** – in many ways, speech, charm, fighting	**Cruel** – unconcerned about causing and distress
Offensive – readily insults and upsets others	**Cowardly** – will sacrifice others to save self	**Solitary** – does not allow others to get close emotionally	**Arrogant** – selfish, but can be overconfident	**Resentful** – envious of others' achievements	**Single-minded** – totally focussed on a goal
Proud – unwilling to admit fault or defeat	**Deluded** – believes what is not true; irrational	**Vengeful** – seeking revenge for supposed wrongs	**Suspicious** – unwilling to trust others	**Controlling** – dominates and manipulates	**Envious** – usually wants what others have got
Crafty – achieves aims through deceit and cunning	**Ashamed** – sometimes hides a past wrongdoing	**Disloyal** – thinks nothing of betraying others	**Boastful** – likes to appear superior to others	**Fanatical** – obsessive about achieving goals	**Knowledgeable** – often has great knowledge
Mysterious – often has hidden depths and intentions	**Immoral** – wicked, untroubled by what is right	**Detached** – showing no sympathy for others	**Clever** – is intelligent, sly, quick-witted	**Charming** – can be pleasant, attentive and attractive	**Predatory** – preys on others' weaknesses

> **Tip** Using a grid means that children can either link ideas randomly using dice rolls or, because all of the information is available at a glance, make creative connections between ideas for themselves.

Activities

- Pick a villain from a story you know. How many of the traits in the grid apply to that character?
- Believable villains often have at least one 'good' quality. Make a list of some that you think would work. Looking at the grid and using the opposite of some of the traits might give you ideas.
- If you were to pick six characteristics from the grid to describe your villain, which would they be and why?
- Create a 'Heroic Traits' grid. Use the opposite qualities from those on the villain grid, plus others from heroes of stories you know.

A narrative template

In many traditional tales, the hero's quest follows a set pattern in terms of the 'ups and downs' of the adventure. Certain key points mark out situations and encounters that fully test the hero's (often hidden) qualities and confirm the character's essential strength, goodness and resilience.

This narrative template can be represented visually –

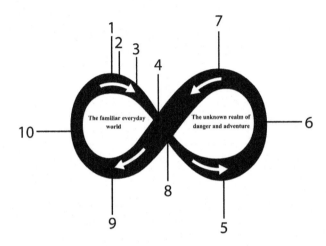

You can explain to the class that the pattern of the story is like a roller coaster ride for the hero, plunging them into challenges and dangers, raising hopes before further crises occur.

Key points of the adventure are –

1. A problem crops up. The hero often doesn't want to get involved.
2. The hero feels duty-bound to help, however, and sets out on the quest.
3. First brush with danger, getting deeper into trouble.
4. A significant encounter with a person, creature etc. that tries to trick or challenge the hero.
5. After further crises and defeats, the hero feels things can't get any worse.
6. Things seem to be getting better ('on the up'), but the hero is far from home, deep inside unfamiliar territory.
7. The hero feels all is well but soon plunges again into difficulty.
8. Further challenges await, but home is on the horizon.
9. A twist in the tale brings a dangerous surprise.
10. But the hero finally overcomes all challenges and normality is restored.

Take it further

The narrative template usually tracks the hero's quest. Once children have a story in mind, suggest that they use the template to follow the villain's journey, a companion's or even a minor character's. This may well lead to further insights into those characters, which may then be more fully developed in the original story or in subsequent ones (Bowkett, 2014; Propp, 2001).

Motifs or tropes

A motif is a constituent feature that helps to describe and define a genre. In fiction, motifs can be people, objects, locations, situations, creatures, snippets of dialogue and concepts. You'll see from the motif grid that some of the ideas will fit any genre, while others are specific to fantasy. As with other grids used in this book, children can simply peruse and choose for themselves, or use dice rolls to select ideas at random. With this grid, children will need to roll two dice at once, two times, in order to select the coordinates of an idea. Note therefore that the coordinates of 'Ladder' are 2/2 (not 1/1), while 'Enchanter', in the top right corner, is 12/12.

Maiden	Guide	Wise One	Prince(ss)	Ruler	Witch	Guardian	Wanderer	Hero(ine)	Beast	Enchanter
Lover	Keeper	Captor	Liberator	Learner	Teacher	Partner	Trial	Quest	Mirror	Blade
Barrier	Road	Gift	Theft	Descent	Ascent	Earth	Air	Fire	Water	Metal
Wood	Stone	Higher	Lower	Chance	Fate	Destiny	Circle	Repeat	Pattern	Chaos
Disguise	Mountain	Pool	Shore	Threshold	Woods	Darkness	Light	Tower	Maze	Bridge
Crossway	Dwelling	City	Gateway	Key	Ocean	Life	Death	Sleep	Wish	Bond
Mother	Father	Sibling	Greater	Lesser	Trickster	Maker	Creature	Tree	Seed	Shoe
Crown	Ball	Talisman	Mark	Colour	Bowl	Weapon	Wand	Crystal	Word	Dance
Number	Moon	Stars	Phases	Time	Edge	Centre	Tangent	Change	State	Betrayal
Egg	Blood	Pact	Dream	Feeling	Game	Goal	Puzzle	Growth	Healing	Opposites
Ladder	Mirror	Origin	Split	Union	Fragment	Wheel	Web	Age	Whole	Unknown

> **Tip** Children can use the grid even if they don't have a single idea in mind for their story. Simply choosing two items (deliberately or randomly) and making a creative connection between them can start the ideas flowing. So –

6/7 Key – 10/2 Growth. A poverty-stricken farmer digs up a key in his field and from that time on begins to prosper. However, there is always a price to be paid...

From that starting point, children can use dice rolls to choose a motif that gives a clue as to what the consequences for the farmer will be, or they can pick an idea deliberately. We rolled 7/11 and got 'Teacher'. The idea came to mind that the key was sent by the gods to teach this farmer or mankind a lesson (reminding us of the story of King Midas, although our farmer is not necessarily greedy).

It's a good idea to use the motifs grid in conjunction with the basic narrative elements and story template that we looked at earlier (pages 35 and 38). Using our seed story, children would need to decide if the farmer is the hero of the story who sets out on a quest, or the villain, or someone caught up in a larger situation affecting the whole country or the world. We reiterate that this grid and our others are designed to kickstart ideas. The primary aim of these and other techniques is to encourage children to ask questions and make decisions, behaviours that form the essence of effective creative writing.

Settings

If writing a high fantasy story, children will need to try and create a logically consistent world (no easy task even for experienced authors!). Alternatively, they can use a world that they have come across in other stories, films etc. Even so, they must be sure that the features of the world and what happens within it are there for good reasons. For instance, one boy we worked with decided that gravity in his world would be half that of Earth. When we asked why, he said that in a film he'd watched, the fight scenes were 'slowed down' and looked more exciting. He had confused a filmic device with a feature of his borrowed world that seemed to be there for no other reason. Rather than deny him his slo-mo action, we suggested that when his hero went into fight mode, because of his quick reflexes everyone else appeared to be moving at half speed. Our hero could even turn aside from a speeding arrow and snatch it out of the air.

A great source of ideas for high fantasy stories is the mythology and folklore of different cultures. Tackling such a story gives children an excellent opportunity for research by revisiting myths and legends you read with them or studying the mythology of a culture they've not looked at before. Children can cherry-pick characters, creatures, plot ideas and settings and build them into a world of their own invention. This is done to inform children of the myths of different lands and so that they may develop as writers. We do not therefore regard this as being tokenistic or disrespectful in any way.

In everyday or low fantasy tales, children can use our familiar world and allow fantasy elements to emerge within it. For us, the fun here is in asking questions such as –

- How can fantasy creatures and people stay hidden from the public or police etc.?
- Why do wizards or dragons or whatever visit this world in the first place?
- How do our fantasy characters interact with modern technology?
- How come characters from the magical world speak the same language as the everyday characters? Or if they don't, how can the language problem be solved?
- Does magic work the same in our world as in the realm where the wizard (or whoever) originates?

A variation of the everyday fantasy idea is to have two-way traffic between our world and a magical realm, where characters from both worlds visit each other's domains. A good example of this is the novel *Elidor* (1972) by Alan Garner.

The fantasy settings grid offers some ideas for locations and landscapes that children might choose for a high fantasy story.

Enchanted Forest	Mountains of Doom	River of Time	Cave of Shadows	Skeleton Coast	Zombie Swamp
Elfin Wood	City of Yesterday	Castle of Death	River of Illusions	The Clashing Rocks	Crystal Henge
Harrowing Stone	Midnight Valley	Dragon Lake	Fairy Dell	Wraithtown	Place of Dreams
Monster Maze	The Vanishing Village	Sea of Oblivion	Pool of Fortune	Valley of the Minotaur	Road of the Dead
Desert of Dread	Wolfenwood	Abyss of Lost Souls	Fountain of Future Events	Harpy Cliffs	Three Wishes Brook
Badlands	The Underworld	Lagoon of Power	Floating Islands	Killer Canyon	Witchdell

Other activities using the grid are –

● Mix and match ideas from the grid to create a greater landscape. Draw a map of the magical realm. Use the narrative template (page 38) to decide how the plot would work within the landscape.

● Play around with our ideas to create new ones. So, Wolfenlake, Skeleton Desert, Cave of Monsters, Castle of Wishes.

● Choose one of the ideas for a setting and **visualise** it in greater detail. What colours, sounds, textures etc. are associated with Wraithtown, for instance?

● Ask searching questions. In what ways are the Badlands bad? What power is associated with the Lagoon of Power? What enchantment is to be found in the Enchanted Forest?

● Vocabulary. Research words such as abyss, dell, harrowing, henge, wraith. Make distinctions. For instance, how is the River of Illusions different from the Place of Dreams?

Story threads

These are deliberately vague statements that act as platforms on which more specific plot ideas can be built. They adhere to the creative principle of 'flexibility within a structure', whereby a certain amount of information is given but the statements themselves can be interpreted in different ways.

Story Threads.

- Effort against the odds.
- A chance surge of energy.
- The heavens bring power.
- Opportunity favours preparedness.
- Beauty in the heart of the beast.
- Achievement may be misinterpreted.
- Kindness translates in many ways.
- Creation evolves.
- Learning may be painful.
- Conditions influence outcomes.
- Energy takes many forms.
- Masks may disguise unexpectedly.
- Disbelief lacks eyes.
- Illusion requires permission.
- Reality is negotiated.
- Payment in kind or not kind.
- Justice is relative.
- Insight comes from more than four quarters.
- Kindness is recognised.
- Gratitude may be unspoken or dumb.
- Thunder dwindles.
- Theft is argued as rightful ownership.
- Consider the consequences of happy accidents.
- Energy forces change.
- Innocence learns one way or another.
- Storms serve many purposes.
- Perseverance focuses energy.
- What rests behind the mask?
- What lies behind the mask?

So, if we take the story thread 'learning may be painful' and use it in the context of a fantasy story, it might mean –

- The hero is taught to use a weapon by the mentor and gets hurt in the process.
- Using magic more artfully brings painful consequences.
- A character needs to tame a wild dragon, and this is not an easy process.
- The villain learns to his or her cost that the worm can turn.
- Retrieving the enchanted amulet means a difficult journey across rough terrain.

Here are some ways of using story threads to help children build a fantasy story – though the technique can also apply to other genres –

- As above, present the class with a story thread and collect as many inter-pretations of the statement as possible. This can also be a group activity. Create a list of statements for each group. Write each statement on a scrap of paper and place them in an envelope to be drawn at random. As with using dice rolls, for the grids to be found elsewhere in this book, 'randomis-ing' the activity develops the spontaneous use of the imagination. This men-tal skill is necessary for generating lots of ideas, which form the raw material that children can then reflect on and refine subsequently.
- Work with the class to create further story threads from books or comics they read or films they watch. The list given here was created as we watched one of the old Hammer Frankenstein films…
- 'Effort against the odds' was Victor Frankenstein's struggle to kindle life in his creature despite the disapproval of friends and colleagues and the hostil-ity of the mob when they discover the nature of his experiments.
- 'A chance surge of energy' and 'The heavens bring power' refer to the bolt of lightning that strikes the metal conductor, so supplying the energy to power Frankenstein's life-bringing apparatus.
- 'Opportunity favours preparedness' refers to the fact that Frankenstein had set up his experiment previously and the machinery was all ready to receive the lightning strike when the storm came.

Obviously, the statements children come up with will most likely not be as 'sophisticated' or abstract as these. Introduce the class to the idea of generali-sation or 'deliberate vagueness' before showing them the list.

Take it further: Here generalised statements are used for a positive, creative purpose. But generalisations are sometimes used negatively, especially in the area of debate/disagreement. As we write this chapter, vitriolic discussion is still taking place across the land between 'Brexiteers' and 'Remainers' with regard to Britain leaving the EU. The emotional charge behind some people's opinions is such that these terms are often modified so as to be insulting. Generalising is not a robust or honest technique within a debate. Once children are aware of it, they can avoid it when writing argumentative essays or during class discus-sions – or use their awareness to point it out as a counter-move and so score a point against the opposition!

For further information see Bowkett (2017, p. 24–27), the dangers of generalising.

Cliché

In creative writing, a cliché is a motif that is overused, and according to Google Dictionary, lacks original thought, while according to the Concise Oxford English Dictionary, it is a 'hackneyed literary phrase'. However, it may be that while a phrase about a character, creature or situation in a child's work may be regarded as a cliché by an adult reader, the idea might be original to that child at that stage in their development. In other words, they've thought of it for themselves for the first time. Furthermore, many writers go through the 'imitation stage' in their development, copying ideas from authors they admire, films they enjoy and so on. So, while we recognise the desire to encourage children towards greater freshness of expression, we would not penalise any child for using a hackneyed idea, especially if it 'does the job' within the context of the story.

Here are some activities around the idea of cliché –

● Show the class a character stereotype and ask the children what changes they could make to give that character a fresh twist. For example –

(a)

Below is a suggestion for 'freshening up' the character…

- Ask children to think of at least one good reason why the wizard should have bird's feet.
- What other changes can the children think of, and how would they help to improve a story?

(b)

- Test the cliché. Many children when they are describing a storm say that the wind 'howled'. First, remind the class that wolves howl, and ask if that is the same sound as the wind. (Some children might say yes to this, so our next move would be to play audio clips of a windy day and of wolves and compare the two. You can take this further by playing audio clips of various wind sounds and asking children to distinguish between them by using different adjectives and verbs, perhaps from a selection you show them.)
- The use of magic. Sometimes it's tempting for children to use magic as an easy way of getting characters out of any tight spot. This is another kind of cliché, and when it's used it suggests first-snatched-thought or lazy thinking. When asking children to plot their stories, suggest that they include at least one restriction on its use. Here are some ideas –

- Challenge 'first thought thinking' at the reviewing stage (see page 105). Rather than interrupting children's creative flow during the first drafting of a story, help them to look at their work more critically when they have finished. Point out clichés by all means, though we would advise a light touch for the reasons mentioned above. Also, it may be that children's use of cliché is the result of limited experience of the genre or of creative writing itself. Sometimes however the use of cliché is simply due to 'lazy thinking' as children grab at the first phrase that pops into mind. This habit inhibits their development as creative writers and so should be challenged.
- Clichés in fantasy fiction. Point out some overused and predictable motifs in fantasy stories and ask the children for ideas about how to 'freshen them up'. Here are some examples of overused ideas –
    1. The prophecy that the 'Chosen One' will appear and save the world.
    2. The wise old wizard.
    3. The Dark Lord.

4. Black/dark is used for evil and light/white is used for good.
5. The 'medieval feel' of the world in a high fantasy story.
6. Names deriving mainly from Finnish/Welsh/Celtic/Norse.
7. The main character wields a sword.
8. Male characters dominate. 'Good' female characters are there to be rescued.
9. Characters miraculously or magically come back to life.
10. All dwarves etc. look the same, while only human characters vary in appearance.
11. A wizard points a wand and energy streams out of it to solve a problem.
12. The King governs the realm (i.e. overuse of monarchies).
13. Elves, dwarves and dragons exist alongside humans.
14. A lack of science and an overuse of alchemy.
15. Medieval technology and/or over-reliance on magic.
16. There must be a quest.

With regard to this last motif, we mentioned earlier that the idea of the quest is central to the narrative template we offered. If you or the children regard it as a cliché, then what other shape could the story be – i.e. not the infinity symbol but…?

Each genre has its own motifs – people, places and objects – though some can overlap. Perhaps when we look at this picture we think of it as a wishing well. This would make it fit nicely into a fantasy story. But what if we wanted to use it as a horror story, or a science fiction or a crime tale? What might have happened to account for what we notice; the partly eaten apple, the overturned basket, the giant mushrooms, the broken rope?

Design a... character, costume, creature, weapon

Look at written or drawn descriptions of characters, costumes, creatures and weapons taken from books or found on the Internet and ask children to modify, mix-and-match etc. to create their own.

Create a weapon

Children can choose items for themselves or randomise the process by rolling a die. In this case, use dice rolls to select two items and see if the combination sparks new ideas. With either method, some combinations will work by suggesting a name and even ideas for the design of a weapon, while others won't. So for instance, a 'fireblade', 'scatterball' and 'stormlance' easily create images in the mind's eye. Some combinations might not initially throw up ideas though are worth keeping since inspiration might come later – 'darksabre', 'netgun' and 'spearchain', for example.

Stone	Rope	Light	Dark	Hurricane	Crystal
Scatter	Glass	Knife	Spark	Blade	Spike
Mist	Bolt	Chain	Lance	Snow	Dream
Point	Mace	Throw	Fire	Disc	Star
Heat	Ice	Sabre	Helmet	Spear	Claw
Ball	Net	Gun	Amulet	Beam	Storm

Here are some visuals that might help children to have some further ideas for weapons or costumes –

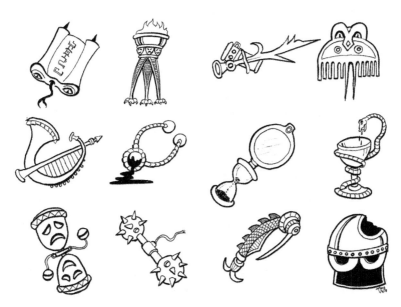

Story starters 1 – Plot ideas

Here are some suggestions for building a fantasy story. Encourage children to change or combine them if they want to –

1. Our character faces danger trying to help the world's last unicorn to survive.
2. The Dark Book of Enchantment is like a labyrinth. You need to be careful and clever to use its power and live.
3. The three fragments of a powerful amulet are hidden in the city where our main characters live. A mage from 'elsewhere' enlists their help in finding them.
4. A race of ruthless wulfen warriors has invaded Midgard. Our hero gets caught up in the conflict between them and the usually peaceful people of that land.
5. An evil spellcaster has come to our world to evade capture. A group of friends finds out about them and helps to track the fugitive down.
6. A child appears as though from nowhere in an ordinary town in our world. People soon discover that somehow he can affect reality and make wishes come true – but with unforeseen consequences.
7. Playing the videogame *The Rise of Annwn* becomes a serious matter when our group of school friends realise their game play is really happening in the parallel realm of Aerth.
8. Three young adventurers compete to free the princess imprisoned in the castle's high tower. But she has been locked up there for a very good reason.
9. Our main character is Fae (a young Faery) who, towards the end of childhood, discovers that they were kidnapped from our world and raised in Summerealm, but now wants to discover why and return home.
10. The Guardian of the House of Forever, which lies on the threshold of many realms, is dying. He must now find a worthy successor to keep the house and the Omniverse safe.

Plot grid. Another method for plotting is to use a 6x6 grid of images. Using dice rolls ('along the corridor and up the stairs'), choose two images at random and link them to generate an idea for what the story will be about.

Follow this up with an open question relating to plot, characters or settings. Then carry out a further dice roll that will answer the question or at least give a clue. Make a note. Proceed by asking further open questions, each one interspersed with dice rolls to provide answers or clues.

Most children, once they have got the hang of the method, find that stories grow 'organically' without struggling to try and have ideas. Frequently children find that the plot completes itself even if dice rolls have only led them part way through the narrative (Bowkett, 2010).

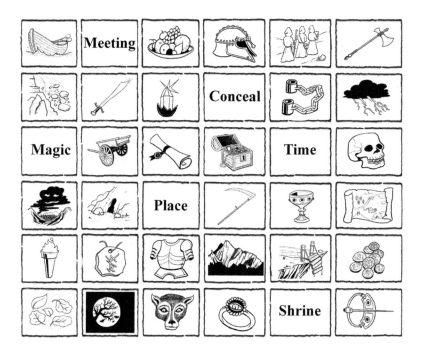

Story starters 2 – Opening paragraphs

1. They had never ventured so far into the woodland. What had been a clear pathway dwindled now to a thin animal track and then petered out entirely. 'I think we'd better turn back', Merion said. The afternoon light was fading and shadows were deepening among the trees. Petra frowned. 'If we do, our journey will have been wasted. Maybe if we go on for just a few more minutes…' But no sooner had the words been spoken than they glimpsed something up ahead and, hurrying, moved towards it. Merion gasped at their good fortune. Yes, there it was, the thing they had been searching for.

2.   Weland came upon the crest of the ridge and scanned the landscape. Yes, there where he had expected: three – four – no, five pale blotches like little puffs of cloud among the deep shadows of the gully.

Weland began to move towards them –

Then something swished by him, as though a bird had flown close past his ear. He looked behind himself but could see nothing. The afternoon's clouds had vanished as the air cooled towards evening: the sky was a glory of deepening blue and violet close to the horizon. He would easily be able to spot some late-roosting blackbird or swallow.

The sound came again, but this time whatever caused it fell to the ground a few paces off to his left. Weland walked over and knelt, sweeping the grass and the bracken with his open hands. He touched feathers, a wooden shaft.

The arrow had flown far; its head had barely penetrated the soil and would have done him no serious harm even if it had struck him. But still, the sight of it filled Weland with alarm.

He crouched down small, screening himself behind the bracken, scanning the horizon. And there – yes, he saw them now – shapes moving swiftly on the opposite slope and more of them, many more, coming quickly over the hill.

3.   By the flickering light of a low-burning fire, the man called Ahab the Guardian wove together the threads of a rug as though his life depended on the task – as indeed it did, together with the lives of all who dwelt within Elyssia.

Outside a battle was raging as Ahab's few remaining followers pitted themselves against the slaves of the dark. They had come unexpectedly out of the forest; nameless things, twisted, warped, blindly following the commands of their master, the Lord of Deceit… Ahab grinned, but there was no humour in his eyes. He would not bring himself to speak the evil one's name, for to do so would give him another particle of strength. And he was powerful enough, that one. Maybe too powerful now to withstand.

4.   The sound of movement never vanished entirely. It ebbed and flowed through the woods as though whoever was making it didn't know the way out. Sometimes the clumping faded almost away, but then would come a heavy crash, branches lashing this way and that, the snap of wood, then the drumming again as the horse searched for a different route to freedom.

That was it, of course! I almost slumped with relief. A horse from one of the local hunt stables must have broken loose and come blundering through Patchley Woods in a panic; the lights were most likely from a Land Rover; men must be all around us trying to catch the animal, trying to stop it bolting and hurting itself –

There were lights again, not the single blistering blaze of a searchlight, but coloured sparkles spiralling deep through the trees. Odd... Car tail-lights, maybe? A fire?

The reds and yellows seemed to gather themselves, then come hurtling between the trees with a fierce crackling that rasped and snapped in the air.

Against the whirlpool of sparks was outlined the shape of a man on a horse, riding expertly, trying to keep to the shadows. But the shower of lights sped closer, moving now towards us.

'Where', Connor asked me, 'is the horse's head?'

5. Berkana crested the hill with Anko and the others close behind. It was almost dawn and the moon was a huge amber disc beyond the Sowelu mountains, swiftly setting between the peaks.

The hunting party had been in pursuit of its prey for two days, but now the chase was coming to an end. The quarry was sure to be exhausted, hungry and frightened. It must know that the time of its death was approaching. And when that time came, perhaps at long last the breed would be finished – pushed over the dark brink of extinction where it belonged. Berkana felt a twinge of regret that things had come to this. But it was for the best: there could not be two dominant species in the land now that Mankind had gone. Even the fleeting thought of it made a picture in Berkana's mind of a bleak future splashed with blood, littered with bones, where the violence and terror of warfare were never-ending. Better that the Night Eyes should go quickly into the dark than for it to suffer any longer or – much worse than this – survive to find a partner and breed.

3 Writing a science fiction story

Summary of the chapter

- Introduction. Defining science fiction and distinguishing between SF, 'space opera' and fantasy. A brief history of SF. Looking at the elements of a short story. Using science fiction as a context for learning more about science and technology, and as a way of developing thinking skills. Considering SF scenarios as metaphors for exploring real-life issues. Exploring how blending SF with other genres can be a stimulus for creative thinking and generating new ideas.
- Aspects of a short story. The five commonly noted aspects are characters, setting, plot, conflict and theme. This chapter features the idea of a 'story pyramid', a visual tool showing how these and genre are related.
  - Characters. Looking at personification in the creation of aliens, robots etc.
  - Plot. Using some plot ideas commonly found in SF to generate further ideas. Also looking at the notion of internal consistency when plotting.
  - Setting. The focus here will be on vivid details and conciseness in writing, including use of strong adjectives and verbs. Structure and function look at how creatures in SF fit into their various environments. The 'World Builder' activity shows how believable SF settings can be created.
  - Conflict. Touching on the notion of strength of reasons and character motivation in the context of conflict.
  - Theme. The emphasis in this section will be on how real-life themes can be used in SF.
- 'A note on nomenclature' touches on the use of the Greek alphabet in naming stars. We take a look at prefixes. There are also techniques for creating SF character names and story titles.

- A medley of thinking games that can be used in any genre – What if/The Merlin game/Thumbnails/Word clouds.
- The chapter finishes with a handful of story starters.

Introduction

Science fiction (also called SF or sci-fi) as a genre uses scientific principles and concepts as a basis for the scenarios it explores. In other words, it has a 'relationship' with science and the technology that science gives rise to. So-called 'hard' SF or nuts-and-bolts science fiction focuses on scientific accuracy and the realistic depiction of future technology based on what is known today. Such technology is central to the structure of the story, such that if the technology element was missing, the story itself could not be told. This approach is sometimes also known as 'the idea as hero', where the central scientific or technological concept takes precedence over other aspects of the story. 'Softer' SF does not necessarily adhere so strictly to physical laws and scientific principles and may use them as dramatic devices just to make the story work. For example, the idea of a teleporter allows characters to move quickly from one place to another, regardless of whether teleportation technology could ever actually exist.

The British writer Bob Shaw has said similarly that a science fiction story is one that contains an element without which the story would collapse. So, for instance, Shaw conceived the idea of 'slow glass'; a substance that slows light down as it passes through. The thickness of the glass determines how long light rays will take to travel from one side to the other. Apparently, Shaw had the idea for slow glass many months before he thought of a way of building it into a plot. His 1966 story 'The Light of Other Days' tells poignantly of a man standing in the rain waiting to catch a glimpse of his dead wife and child, whose images when still alive were captured in the glass, at some point to emerge on the other side. That story incidentally forms part of Shaw's novel *Other Days, Other Eyes*, which explores the impact of slow glass on society. (We'll come back to slow glass in the 'What if' activity on page 80).

Space opera is considered to be a subgenre of SF and focuses on adventures set in outer space that are usually epic in nature, dealing with galactic empires and wars between confederations of planets, for example. It is linked to what has been called 'space Westerns', stories that take the *motifs* (tropes) and *conventions* of the Wild West and use them in a science fictional setting. Some commentators distinguish between science fiction and science fantasy, which contains a mystical or supernatural element not explained by science. The 'force' in the Star Wars universe is a well-known example of a science fantasy motif.

The SF writer Isaac Asimov is quoted as saying that science fiction grounded as it is in science is possible, whereas fantasy is not possible since it has no link with reality. This definition might be challenged, given that SF can be used **allegorically**. H. G. Wells's *The Time Machine*, for instance, concerns itself with the way that human beings in the far future have split into two species, the sybaritic Eloi who live in luxury above ground and the spidery Morlocks who labour in subterranean factories to produce the food and clothes that the Eloi enjoy and rely on; an arrangement that comes at a terrible cost. Wells's story is a cautionary tale whose theme is the extreme inequality in terms of wealth and opportunity that existed between the upper and working classes of late Victorian society in Britain. So, although time machines may never be possible, Wells's tale does concern itself with real-life issues. (Beyond that, stories that everyone would classify as fantasy can and do derive some of their power as narratives by dealing with relationships and conflicts that mirror those existing in the real world.)

If you read *The Time Machine*, you may find, as we did, that Wells's description of how the time machine works is very convincing. The time traveller's explanation is an example of what is called pseudo-science (also known as technobabble), which, when it is done well, allows the reader to suspend disbelief and 'buy into' the premise of the story. The poet Samuel Taylor Coleridge coined the term 'suspension of disbelief' in 1817, and it is nowadays taken to mean the willingness of an audience or readership to accept the events and characters in a story that otherwise would be seen as incredible. In this regard, good fantasy has been described as making the impossible seem possible, while good science fiction makes the possible seem probable.

What has been termed 'proto science fiction' can be traced back almost two thousand years to when Lucian of Samosata in his *True History* wrote of a man who travelled into the heavens and witnessed a battle between the People of the Moon and the People of the Sun. Similarly, *One Thousand and One Nights*, a collection of Middle Eastern folk tales, contains many motifs that today would be called SF, such as a man-made horse that with the turn of a key can pull a cart to carry people beyond the atmosphere, and a city filled with automata.

Some people credit Mary Shelley's *Frankenstein* as opening the modern era of science fiction (though the story can also be seen as Gothic horror), while others say that later writers such as Edgar Allan Poe, H. G. Wells and Jules Verne, with their wonderful scientific romances, began to define what today is one of the richest and most diverse genres in literature.

Interestingly, and possibly having some connection with 'romance' in the context of SF, the educationalist Kieran Egan formulated the Cognitive Tools Theory in the 1990s. Simply put, Egan postulates that we progress through five kinds of understanding as we grow, and that between the ages of 8 and 14, people exhibit what he calls a 'romantic understanding' of the world. This is characterised by a childlike sense of wonder but also a desire to explore the limits and boundaries of human potential – a definition that fits rather well what much of what more serious SF endeavours to achieve (Egan, 1997).

Aspects of a short story

Characters

While the aim of all the sections in this book is to help children write crea-tively across a range of genres, those genres can also be used as contexts for exploring knowledge and ideas in different subject areas. There are sections elsewhere in this book about developing characters (see our checklist of top-ics), so here we want to offer a few ideas that look at personification within the context of the non-human type characters routinely found in SF stories.

1. If necessary, explain the notion of **personification**, then work with the class to compile a list of SF characters that have one or more human-like qualities. These may be positive or negative, depending on whether a character is 'on the side of the good guys' or is villainous. Then ask the children to consider these questions –

    – What **specific** characteristics in the examples collected fit the defini-tion of personification? For example, humanoid body shape, a sense of humour, loyalty to a friend, human-like facial expressions etc.

    – Leading on from the first question and looking at the famous droids from the Star Wars movies, is C3PO more human-like than R2D2? What characteristics of R2D2 lead us to call him (it?) a 'character'? Is Chewbacca the Wookie more human-like than the droids? (Incidentally, the word character comes from the Greek meaning 'a stamping tool', something that leaves a distinguishing mark. The idea evolved into the sense of distinguishing traits and qualities.)

Note: We are picking examples that hopefully most children will have heard of, if not seen in the films themselves (given their age rating). There are many video clips available online, though again permissions may be required to allow children to view them.

2.   How could a creature that is utterly non-human in form be personified so that it (he? she?) becomes the hero's companion in a science fiction story? In other words, invent a companion that is non-human, but that even so has been personified and can feature as a character.

3.   Why are vehicles such as cars personified by being given the female gender, do you think? Why do we still speak of 'Mother Earth' when referring to our home world? (See the reference Quora.com for an interesting take on this.)

4.   If computers ever became conscious, would you be happy to have one as a friend? If not, what qualities or characteristics would you want it to have before you felt you could befriend it? Or do you think you could never make friends with an intelligent machine (having given some thought to what 'intelligence' means)?

Note: If you are pursuing a philosophical thinking skills agenda in your classroom, here's an opportunity for the children to discuss whether consciousness and intelligence are the same thing; whether one depends on the other; whether artificial intelligence (AI) implies consciousness; and whether this would be the same as human consciousness. For more ideas around philosophy for children (P4C), see Bowkett, 2018; Buckley, 2011; and Fisher, 2004 in the 'References' section.

5.   Whether you like the Daleks in Doctor Who or not, they are enormously popular with viewers of the programme. Why do you think this might be?
6.   Either make a list of the features and characteristics you would use to create a new alien (but personified) character in a science fiction story... Or, what changes would you make to a standard Dalek to create a newer and deadlier version?

Plot

Here are some ideas commonly used in SF plots, together with a few variations on each. Ask the children if they can think of any further alternatives.

- Robots. Disobeying humans/going out of control/becoming more intelligent than humans. (Also check out Isaac Asimov's famous Three Laws of Robotics if you want the children to think of more sophisticated variations on these common robot themes.)

Note: In fiction, robots and androids are more or less the same thing, except that androids tend to be given a more human appearance. The word android comes from the Greek *andro* meaning 'man' and the suffix *–oid* meaning 'like' (see 'Prefixes and suffixes' on page 77). Technically, then, R2D2 and C3P0 are robots, not 'droids'. 'Robot' incidentally comes from the Czech word *robota*, meaning 'forced labour', and was coined in Karel Čapek's 1920 play *R.U.R.* (*Rossum's Universal Robots*). A cyborg, on the other (mechanical?) hand, is part human and part machine. The word, coined in the 1960s, is short for 'cybernetic organism'. 'Cyber' relates to the world of computers, digital technology generally and virtual reality (VR).

● Interstellar Travel. Meeting alien species/wars between alien races or aliens and humans/discovering amazing alien technology and its consequences/ discovering parallel Earths – like our world but with interesting differences/ use of 'portals' to travel instantaneously to many distant worlds, and consequences that may result from this.

Note: Opportunities exist here to discuss colonialism and the issue of differences and similarities between human cultures. The word 'alien' comes from the Latin *alienus*, meaning 'belonging to another', and before referring to creatures from outer space was used more generally to mean 'foreigner' or 'stranger'. A number of SF stories use issues between humans and aliens as **allegories** commenting on conflicts between cultures in the real world. A related issue is what in the Star Trek universe is known as the Prime Directive, which is the intention not to interfere with alien cultures (although of course this rule is almost always broken or ignored in the series, otherwise plots would be very thin on the ground!).

● Time travel. Going back in time to try and change history/travelling back in time to meet yourself/bringing future technology back to the present, to gain power or for other purposes/going into the future to learn something that will benefit you now/future humans coming back to our present, for various reasons.

Note: Time travel as an aspect of SF stories raises the famous time paradox, viz. what if you built a time machine, went back into the past and accidentally caused the death of your grandparent before your mother/father was born? That means you would not exist. Therefore, you could not have built your time machine. But if that were the case, you could not have caused your grandparent's death, which means you *would* have existed to build your machine, go back into the past and accidentally caused the death of your grandparent... One way out of this paradox is to postulate the idea of parallel timelines, so that in one timeline you did cause the death of a grandparent, but that 'tweaked' you into a parallel timeline where you continue to exist.

Some time travel stories also explore the 'butterfly effect'. This is a term used in chaos theory and means that a tiny action can cause larger consequences down the line. The notion is that a butterfly fluttering its wings in one part of the world triggers a ripple effect that eventually results in a hurricane on the other side of the globe – i.e. tiny starting conditions can lead to huge, unpredictable consequences.

A famous butterfly-effect story is Ray Bradbury's 'A Sound of Thunder'. In this, the company Time Safaris Inc. offers customers the chance to go back millions of years to hunt T. rex and other predatory dinosaurs. Each hunt is carefully planned: the dinosaur to be hunted would have died anyway shortly afterwards through natural causes, so there would be no unforeseen consequences. A metal path guides the hunters to the kill spot and the golden rule is that you must not step off the path. One of the characters however accidentally does this and inadvertently crushes a butterfly, so that upon his return he finds the world to be a very different place. Audio versions are available on YouTube.

Logical consistency

We've already touched on the fact that well-written SF (and fantasy) stories need to be believable. They are not 'anything goes' kinds of stories, and as such are not the easiest options to tackle. One way of making stories within these and other genres more robust is to make them logically consistent. This means that certain 'rules' need to apply throughout. Suppose, for instance, that you wrote about a world where the gravity was the same as that of our Moon (about one-sixth of Earth's). On that world, a human explorer would weigh less than on Earth and would be able to jump higher (through having the same muscular strength), but they would not be able to jump over mountains. So, to have a character moving along a la the famous Apollo astronauts' 'kangaroo hops' but then leaping many metres in the air to avoid pursuing aliens would not be logically consistent.

At this level, the idea is quite sophisticated, but you can explain it to the children by saying, for instance, that if a character has blue eyes at the start of the story, she must have blue eyes at the end – though if the colour does change it must be for a good reason that supports the logic of the story (maybe she is wearing amazing blue contact lenses that allow her to see one minute into the future. Now there's an idea for a story!).

- Superpowers. Suddenly gaining superpowers and the consequences of that/powers that wax and wane/powers that change the owner's personality/ teaming up with other 'superpersons'.

Plotting stories about superpowers creates the opportunity for children to think about logical consistency, insofar as they will need to consider beforehand the strengths and weaknesses of their characters. One easy way of doing this is to prepare a character sheet like this for each super-character and ask children to fill these in before planning the story in detail (the template, suitably modified, can be used in other genres). Note also that the most believable superheroes have at least one weakness, such as Superman's vulnerability to kryptonite.

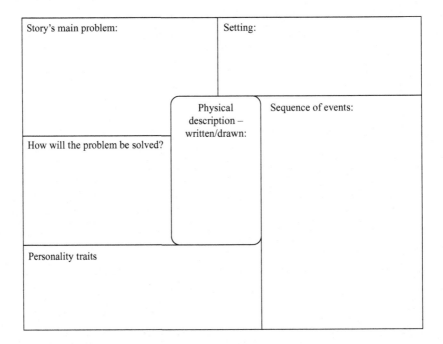

Such stories are also great 'arenas' for children to write fast-paced action scenes with plenty of spectacular special effects, although some young writers might prefer to focus more on what it feels like actually to be a superhero, but with 'real-world' problems – which is why for us, Spider-Man (especially in the earlier comic stories) is believable, insofar as he catches colds, struggles to make enough money, worries about his elderly Aunt May (in the comics and earlier films) and struggles with his lack of confidence in asking Gwen Stacy out on a date.

In creating superheroes and villains you can also refer to the noble and mean qualities of such characters to be found on page 37.

● Bodily transformations. This is linked to the idea of superpowers but also includes literal physical changes mirroring different aspects of the psyche, the template for the notion being Robert Louis Stevenson's *The Strange Case of Dr. Jekyll and Mr. Hyde*. The raison d'être for the story might simply be to explore the emotions of the character(s) being transformed and the consequences for society. There is also an overlap with Gothic horror if we consider transformations of people into wolfpeople, into vampires and so on. At a deeper level, transformation stories can be used to explore themes such as alienation and what makes us human.

- Parallel universes. This aspect of SF posits one or more universes that mirror our own to a greater or lesser extent, where differences in physics, biology, history etc. form the basis for a 'what if' kind of story. Perhaps the earliest parallel universe story is *Flatland*, written in 1884 by Edwin Abbott Abbott (*sic*). Here Abbott posits the idea of a truly two-dimensional world and how one of its inhabitants – a square – tries to imagine worlds with a greater number of dimensions. The story itself is a satirical commentary on the hierarchical and unequal nature of Victorian society (note that it was written at almost the same time as Wells's *The Time Machine*, see page 56).

A more modern take on the theme is the 1967 Star Trek episode 'Mirror Mirror', where Captain Kirk and the rest of the landing party are transported to a totalitarian cosmos where the mirror-crew of the Enterprise are evil and brutal.

Parallel universe stories provide an interesting context for children not only to develop their imaginations and creative writing skills but also to place actual knowledge of physics, biology, geography, history etc. into the engaging context of a story. See the 'What if' section on page 79 for more ideas.

- Alien invasion. Evil aliens invade and attempt to conquer Earth/benign aliens take over the world for our own good/aliens emerge from seed pods and look exactly like any human that happened to be nearby (as in the classic 1956 American film – and remakes – *Invasion of the Body Snatchers*)/evil or benign aliens attempt to control our evolution. And extending the idea a little, invasions of giant creatures: insects, monsters from another dimension etc.

Alien invasion stories (we're thinking particularly of 1950s American movies) sometimes reflect a cultural fear of the spread of Communism and also of the unforeseen effects of nuclear radiation – ants, spiders and other creepy crawlies mutating to giant size to terrorise U.S. citizens. H. G. Wells's classic 1887 novel *War of the Worlds*, where super-intelligent hostile Martians invade Earth, wagged a finger at British imperialism and the complacency of the late-Victorian upper classes. The 1953 movie of the same name vividly depicts the increasingly desperate attempts by humanity (including, ironically, the use of a nuclear bomb) to destroy the implacable Martian march across the globe. For comments on its age rating, if you wanted to show it to Year 5/6, check the commonsensemedia.org website in the 'Reference' section.

- Immortality. The notion of living forever, or at least for hundreds or thousands of years, is perhaps the secret wish of many people. But would it be a gift or a curse? Oscar Wilde's *The Picture of Dorian Gray* (1890) is a powerful exploration of the implications of never growing old.

You might consider discussing the idea with the children perhaps using the what-if technique (page 79). Questions can include –

- What if I could 'steal time' from people, so that if I stole ten years from someone I'd stay at my present age for the next ten years, but the other person would immediately age by ten years?
- And what if I could steal time to give to my family and friends? Would I do it?
- What if other people had the same power? Would there be 'time wars' where enemies tried to destroy each other by stealing all the time they had left?

There's an obvious bridge from posing questions like these to more philosophical discussions on the morality of such a power (and by inference, of other actual influences some people can have over others).

Immortality stories are not easy to write in our opinion, insofar as new angles on the theme require great ingenuity, though stories might grow out of the questions above. A linked theme, and one that appears in other genres, is the idea of 'you get nothing for nothing' – whatever you gain, someone somewhere must pay the price.

- The future. Since the earliest days of SF, stories have speculated about what the future of Earth and of humanity might be like. Some writers are optimistic: Thomas More's 1516 story *Utopia* depicted an island paradise where people lived a thoroughly good, monastic kind of existence. The term became more generalised to mean any perfect or ideal place or society, although the word itself, from the Greek, meaning 'not place' or 'nowhere', suggests that More thought utopia was not in fact attainable. The opposite state, a dystopian culture, has been extensively explored in SF – see for instance utopian and dystopian fiction in Wikipedia. Linked to the dystopian subgenre in SF is the notion of a post-apocalyptic world, where nuclear war, epidemics and the like wipe out most of the human race, and those who are left struggle to survive.

Utopian/dystopian stories, however, form just a small section of science fiction books, films and comics that explore possible futures. The writer Arthur C. Clarke wrote both fictional accounts and considered predications based on fact. Clarke was a great optimist, believing that technological progress would allow humanity to flourish both on Earth, throughout the solar system and across the galaxy.

In asking children to think about possible futures, you might try the following –

- Play the 'Merlin game' (page 80) in thinking about how computers, vehicles, food production and other aspects of the modern world might develop in the future.
- Do some research to prepare a timeline of important discoveries and inventions of the past several decades. Extend the timeline to estimate when (or if) things might happen, such as: extensive use of **nanotechnology**, humans landing on Mars, contact with an alien civilisation, truly intelligent machines, human cloning, control of the weather, anti-gravity, memory playback at will, space drives (near light speed or faster than light – FTL – engines), artificial life. (See Clarke's *Profiles of the Future* (2000) for much more.)

Note that most if not all of these ideas can form the basis for stories the children might want to tackle. Another technique is to look at age-appropriate SF movies, TV episodes and comics and ask the children to write stories based upon them. There are also some story starters and plot ideas at the end of this section.

Setting

The universe is your oyster when it comes to creating a setting for a science fiction story. Our experience has been that most children aren't too concerned about the scientific accuracy of places where the action is located. We think that's fine, though it is worth touching upon the importance of logical consistency within a story (see page 31) and perhaps pointing out scientific inaccuracies *after* the work has been completed – not that children will need to edit their work accordingly, but just for their information. For instance, and influenced perhaps by Star Wars and other movies, many children write about thunderous explosions as spacecraft are destroyed by laser cannons (or more generically 'beam weapons') and how the hero in his star cruiser veers away from enemy counterfire just in the nick of time. However, because there is no air in space (no one can hear you scream), sound waves have no medium to travel through, so you couldn't hear any explosions.

As for our hero 'swerving away' in his spacecraft, that violates Newton's first law of motion, which states that a body continues in a state of rest or uniform motion in a straight line unless it is acted on by an external force. In other words, to change direction the pilot needs to cancel motion in the current direction, orient the spacecraft to point the way he wants to go, then apply thrust to propel the ship in that direction. Time-consuming, cumbersome and not very dramatic, but that's physics for you.

Of course, all of this may sound a little pompous, and we repeat that technical details shouldn't inhibit children from writing. So, they can ignore technical details like this or more creatively use technobabble (page 56) to make the story *sound* believable – think for instance of the warp speed, impulse drive and dilithium crystals used in Star Trek or, satirically, the infinite improbability drive invented by Douglas Adams in *The Hitchhiker's Guide to the Galaxy*. One child we worked with showed comparable inventiveness with the 'go-anywhere-now' button he built into the console of his hero's spaceship, allowing us to give him credit for that even though (as yet) it's a physical impossibility.

To give short stories more impact, advise the children to use vivid details and to be concise in their writing. A vivid detail should ideally –

- Create a striking image in the reader's imagination.
- Have some emotional impact (which may be simply an appreciation of the phrase or sentence itself).

Astronaut Edwin 'Buzz' Aldrin, the second man to walk on the Moon, described the lunar landscape as one of 'magnificent desolation', which for us evokes a sense of wonder looking at what is otherwise a rather bland and featureless wilderness of pale rocks and dust. More melodramatically, the writer Edgar Rice Burroughs (creator of Tarzan) wrote a series of SF/fantasy potboilers featuring the swashbuckling hero John Carter. The action is set on Mars (which Burroughs calls Barsoom), and mention is often made of Barsoom's twin moons 'hurtling through the sky'. In fact, while the movement of Mars' moons Phobos and Deimos would be noticeable from the ground, they would hardly be hurtling. That said, the use of such a strong verb reflects the fast pace and drama that Burroughs aims for throughout his stories.

- Show the class this list of vivid sentences, some of which already suggest a location. Ask the children to decide on a setting (not necessarily SF) based on one or more of the sentences and then write a short paragraph describing the place more fully. They can include characters if they wish.
  - The sparkling river rushed beneath tall golden cliffs.
  - Thundering waters surged into the grim and mysterious cave.
  - Phosphorescent rocks glowed with startling purples, greens and reds.
  - Mist swirled in ghostly veils around the towering building ahead.
  - The scales of the creature looked like leaves of hammered bronze.
  - The blade flashed in the dimness, swung wide and clattered against the wall.
  - Heat radiated up from the sun-blasted sands of the desert.
  - I ran through a valley of crystals beneath an astonishing amber sky.
  - Waves curled and crashed upon the shore, hurling sea spray high in the air.
  - A deep roaring rumble signalled the landslide. Then the ground began to shudder.
  - We sped over a tree-dotted plain where countless exotic animals roamed.
  - A slim shaft of white light became a blaze of sunlight as we flung open the outer door.
- Once children have created their descriptive paragraphs you can –
  - Suggest other/better adjectives, verbs and adverbs than the ones we've used.
  - Pick some strong vocabulary from our selection and use the words in other sentences of their own.
  - Get them to plan out the rest of the story (swapping with each other if they like).
  - Look at images of striking landscapes and individually, in pairs or groups, discuss then write a vivid description of the chosen place.
- Create an association web around a setting as a way of generating strong words and vivid phrases. Remember: sights, sounds, smells and textures. Here's one focusing on a cityscape. You may wish to make copies for children to add their own vocabulary –

mirror-like lakes   green parks speckled
with rainbow flowers

towers, glass and steel

Other Features

Skyline   lowering clouds

slow stately grey river

glowing domes green, blue, gold

blazing sunsets, cloud-mountains
of pink and gold

streets thronged with people

complex   bustling

City

noisy   exciting

constant din of machines

thunderous roar of planes

Traffic   harsh growl of motorbikes

trains clattering on tracks

crowds surging

sirens wailing   ## People

milling like ants

swirls of colour -
faces, clothing

sun blasted pavements

Weather

rain drenched streets   rain glittering -
neon lights

● Invite children to write a descriptive paragraph of this alien cityscape –

Structure and function

We've noted how writers of hard SF take pains to make the technology in their stories as accurate and realistic as possible. So too do some authors try to make their work more believable by carefully crafting their planetary settings, fitting the inhabitants of their alien worlds to the landscape and global conditions. While it's not necessary to overburden children by insisting they try this too, the idea does create the opportunity to show how animals and plants have evolved on Earth to maximise their chances of survival. In other words, structure is related to function in the name of 'the survival of the fittest' (which is to say, how organisms are best fitted to survive in their environment).

If you want to develop this point, show children pictures/video clips of a variety of plants and animals and pose questions that ask them to think about the reasons behind form, size, colour and so on…

● Why do giraffes have such long necks?
● Why do many species of cacti have thick waxy skins?
● Why do cats have whiskers?
● Why do dandelion seeds have fluffy tops?
● Why do zebras have stripes while other kinds of horses don't?

Note: What we're aiming at here is to get the children to try and work out *possible* answers to these questions; i.e. we want them to **reason** and **speculate**. For this activity it's not important if they think they know or don't know the right answer.

Extend the activity into the field of SF by showing them these visuals of planetary landscapes and alien creatures (see page 58). Ask them, using the same reasoning, to match each kind of creature with its home world.

World Builder

Show the children the visual and ask the class these questions –

- What colours do you imagine would be in the picture?
- What sounds might you hear?
- What words could you use to describe the landscape and weather?
- What might be the strange device beside the girl?
- If she's holding a smartphone, how might it be better than the phones we have today?

Extend the activity by making copies of the 'World Builder' sheets. Split the class into groups and ask them to devise a world that they could use as the setting for a science fiction story. Children can start from scratch or might want to use the girl-and-jet-car illustration, or an example from page 58.

World Builder:

1) Decide if your world is Earth. If so, the action of the story could be set in the past, now, or some time in the future.

2) If your world is Earth in the future, decide how far ahead.
   How is this future Earth different from today's world?
   Think about climate, ecology, population, technology.

3) If your world is not Earth, decide if it's an actual planet in the Solar System.
   If so, do some research and note down a few facts that will help you to write your story.
   If it's a planet that you are inventing, decide on the following –

a) Size (and therefore gravity).

b) How far from parent star.

c) How many moons, if any.

d) Climate and weather.

e) The intelligent races (if any) that inhabit your world.

f) If so, what level of technology have they reached?

g) Are there any historical events that are important to your story?

h) Think about other plants and animals living on your world, if this is relevant to your story.

i) And the name of your world is?

Use the space below to note down your ideas.

Conflict

Conflict is vital in a story as it drives the narrative and provides motivation for the characters, which in turn delivers an emotional impact to the reader. The most basic type of conflict in a story is person versus person: conflict between the protagonist (hero) and the antagonist (villain). Other kinds of conflict exist, however, and children might choose to feature more than one in a story –

1. Person versus society.
2. Person versus nature.
3. Person versus technology/science.
4. Person versus self.
5. Person versus 'other forces', including fate, aliens or the supernatural.

Ask children to think of examples for each kind of conflict.

Strength of reasons

Another aspect of the believability of a story is the reasons that drive characters to do what they do, i.e. the rationales behind their motivations. Looking at SF specifically, to evoke an evil mad scientist who wants to destroy the world *because* he is evil and mad is the flimsiest kind of reason. While conflict between hero and villain is a necessary aspect of a story, to have them do battle simply because one is good and the other bad is not enough.

One way to help children think more deeply about the reasons underpinning the conflict in their stories is to offer examples of conflict situations (and also get children to come up with some) and ask them to brainstorm possible reasons behind each, then to rate each reason on a 1–6 scale of 'convincingness'.

For example, aliens invade the Earth because –

- They are evil.
- Their home world is about to be destroyed.
- They got bored.
- They need Earth's natural resources.
- Earth is just a stepping-stone to galactic domination.
- They are searching for a super-criminal that may be hiding on Earth.
- An ancient Earth race (Atlanteans?) once invaded their world, so this is revenge.
- They are dying out and need to inhabit human bodies.

Ideas for conflict situations can be based around –

- Self-sacrifice.
- Ambition.
- Family.
- Competitiveness.
- Love.

- Revenge.
- Misjudgement.
- Betrayal.
- Rivalry.
- Injustice.
- Political, religious, racial and other differences.

> **Tip** Children will likely have further ideas for specific examples of conflict under these headings by looking at their favourite films, books and comics. You might also look at the motifs grid in the fantasy chapter on page 39 – choosing items randomly with dice rolls, how could any of the items chosen be used to cause conflict in a story?

Theme

The central conflicts and themes of a story are intertwined. If conflict between characters is based on betrayal, for instance, then per se betrayal is the major theme of the story, followed perhaps by rivalry, revenge and others.

If the basic narrative elements (see page 35) are the building blocks of a story, then themes are the foundations on which they stand. The story pyramid illustrates this.

Level of
individual
stories

Motifis and conventions

Genre

Sub-elements

Basic narrative
elements

Narrative template

Themes

Human condition - level
of all stories

- Human condition. All stories are based on human experience. Fiction remains a valid and important way of expressing our fears, desires and dreams.
- Themes. The big ideas and emotional forces emerging from our experience of life.
- Narrative template. The pattern of good versus evil that will always exist locked in eternal struggle. See page 38.
- Basic narrative elements. Hero, villain, problem and others forming the building blocks of story. See page 35.
- Sub-elements. Variations of how the basic elements are used. The hero is disguised, a false hero appears, the hero is betrayed etc. Although there are a number of traditional sub-elements, children can create their own. See Bowkett, 2009 and Propp, 2001.
- Genre. From the French 'kind', as in a kind or style of literature.
- Motifs and conventions. Motifs are the people, places, objects and events that help to define and describe a genre. Conventions refers to the way that motifs are usually or conventionally used within a given genre.
- All of the above support the structure and 'texture' of individual stories.

Another metaphor that might help children to understand the rather abstract idea of 'theme' is to say that themes are like a river full of swirling currents, and that stories are like leaves being carried along on the surface. The themes control and direct the stories just as the currents in a river determine the movement of the leaves. While every leaf is different and each follows its own path, all the leaves are being carried along in the same basic direction – because we will always need heroes to resolve the problems of evil and injustice (see the Basic Narrative Template on page 35).

A note on nomenclature

Traditionally the letters of the Greek alphabet are used to rank stars in order of their apparent brightness within a constellation (though there are exceptions). So Alpha Centauri, for example, is the brightest star in the constellation of Centaurus the Centaur, and one of the nearest stars to Earth. In recent years several thousand planets have been discovered orbiting stars other than our sun. They are termed exoplanets because they lie outside our own star system. Conventionally they are named by taking the name of the parent star and adding a lowercase letter. Alpha Centauri is a binary system (two stars orbiting one another), and in 2012 astronomers announced that they had discovered a planet orbiting the smaller of the stars, Alpha Centauri B, so the planet was labelled Alpha Centauri Bb. Its existence has since been disputed, however.

Telling the children these facts opens up several opportunities –

- To gain insights into the Greek alphabet (the word 'alphabet' itself derives from the first two letters, alpha and beta) and how Greek has contributed greatly to the development of English.
- Using examples like exo- and bi- to introduce or revisit prefixes and etymology more generally.
- Researching the stories behind constellations, linking this with the study of myths and legends from other cultures.
- Pointing out that in science, many facts are provisional and liable to change. After the announcement of the discovery of Alpha Centauri Bb, further examination of the original study suggested that the planet might instead be an artefact of the way the data were processed.
- Star names and the names of exoplanets can add colour and a sense of realism to SF stories. Who could fail to be impressed if a starship was using its FTL (faster than light) drive to zoom towards 51 Pegasi b, 47 Ursae Majoris c or Tau boötes b?

Character names

An important principle in creative writing is that 'we need to have many ideas to have our best ideas'. With this in mind, one way of generating character names for SF and fantasy stories is to take an ordinary word and scramble the letters in various ways. Some of the rearrangements won't work, but others will, producing cool-sounding names that the children can use. So, out of 'break' we get Rebak, Kaber, Rabek, Abrek, Kebra – all of which are usable, in our opinion. Others are –

Petal – Latep, Talep, Altep.
Brave – Vaber, Raveb, Bevra.
Cloud – Codul, Duloc, Culod.
Rattan – Tarran, Narrat, Arrant.

Another technique is to play around with ordinary names by scrambling, adding or deleting letters and trying different spellings. So out of Brian we get – Brin,

Bran, Rian, Nira; Nigel – Ligen, Glien, Glin, Ingel; Steve – Steev, Sev, Vees, Teves, Veet.

This activity is not frivolous for the reason we've given above, but also it is a form of wordplay that encourages mental agility and helps children to understand the idea of puns and repartee; aspects of what has been called 'cultural literacy'.

Prefixes

Wordplay using prefixes, suffixes and roots can generate ideas for new SF motifs while boosting children's vocabulary by giving them insights into where some of our words come from. (For instance, we discovered that 'astronaut' derives from the Latin *astro*, meaning 'star', and *nauta*, 'sailor'. An astronaut is a sailor to the stars, a vivid and poetical idea.)

Below is a list of some prefixes children can use to generate new ideas.

- Give a few examples of how the prefixes are used ordinarily – anti-theft paint, automobile, binary (stars, numbers etc.), bisect and so on. Help the children to further understand these terms by asking questions such as –
  - In what sense is the paint 'against' theft?
  - What does 'mobile' mean? So, an automobile is…?
  - The word 'sect' means cut, cut off or separate. The word 'bisect' means to cut into two. How do these ideas help us to understand words like section, sector, dissect, insect, intersection?
- Help the children to do some wordplay by combining the prefixes with the following words. Ask the children which terms work and what image they have in their mind's eye: car, bot (as in robot), drive, droid, ship, weapon.

Anti – against.
Auto – self.
Bi/bis – two.
Cyber – controlled by machines (originally from the Greek for 'steersman').
Deca – ten.
Ex – out of, from.
Hyper – beyond, above.
Inter – between.
Mal – bad.

Meta – change.
Mono – one, alone.
Octo – eight.
Omni – all, universal.
Para – beside.
Pseudo – false.
Retro – backwards.
Super – above, greater than.
Ultra – beyond.

Some great answers from children include –

Cybercar – a car that directs itself.
Decabot – a robot with many functions/a robot with ten arms.
Hyperdroid – an android that's better than all others.
Metaship – a spaceship that can turn into other machines (like the Transformers).
Omnidrive – a spaceship that can take you anywhere.
Retrobot – a robot that can go back in time.
Ultragun – More powerful than all other handheld weapons.

Story titles

Mixing and matching can also throw up some fresh ideas for the titles of SF stories. Often, the title will lead to further plot ideas, for example 'Guardian at the End of Time', 'Mutant Wars' or 'Mission to the World of Shadows' (see the second Story Title Grid).

The children don't have to cross match a word from a column and one from a row: playing with just the words in the columns or those in the rows can also produce results. Encourage the use of the definite and indefinite articles, conjunctions and prepositions, singular and plural terms and trying the words out as different parts of speech. Some thoughts from young writers include: Robot City, Battle World, Odyssey Through Time, Empire Troopers, The Deserted Moon, The Time Portal, War of the Empires, Lost Aliens, Alien Empire, Robots Attack.

Mutants	Invasion	Stars	Aliens	Robots	Legion	City	World	Galactic	Battle	Empire	Time
War											
Troopers											
Moon											
Odyssey											
Planet											
Portal											
Attack											
Lost											
Return											
Space											
Deserted											

Extend the activity by inviting children to fill in the empty cells with further vocabulary, and/or they can work with our example. Most children will have ideas readily just glancing at the grid; all of the words are 'visually available', constantly in view, and our minds naturally try to make connections by putting previously separate ideas together to create further meaning. Alternatively, children can use 12-sided dice to generate ideas at random – bearing in mind the principle that 'to have our best ideas we need to have many ideas'.

Mutants	Invasion	Stars	Aliens	Robots	Legion	City	World	Galactic	Battle	Empire	Time
War	Colony	Monsters	Shield	Final	Chase	Jewels	Child	Infinity	Bridge	Fall	Mission
Troopers	Aftermath	Encounter	Clouds	Beyond	Forest	Fire	Destiny	Force	Killing	First	Tomb
Moon	Warrior	Veil	Unknown	Comet	Edge	Games	Inferno	Rebellion	Power	Orbit	Keeper
Odyssey	Zone	Doom	Future	Citadel	Mind	Fear	King	Journey	Menace	Android	Silent
Planet	Creature	Legend	Revenge	Prince	Adventure	Clones	Night	Thief	Trap	Nebula	Land
Portal	Guardian	Sea	Base	End	Trials	Million	Parallel	Machine	Shadows	Mask	Slayer
Attack	Lair	Paradise	Shield	Traveller	Cyborg	Omega	Tomorrow	Sword	Cosmic	Seeds	Experiment
Lost	Ocean	Last	Crystal	Echoes	Gods	Stones	Warlord	Forbidden	Enemy	Gate	Twilight
Return	Ice	Eternal	Light	Evil	Frontier	Rings	High	Invisible	Morning	Dream	Storm
Space	Earth	Shield	People	Nowhere	Sky	Oblivion	Curse	Helix	Hunter	Mists	Unknown
Deserted	King	Darkness	Genesis	Ship	Burning	Beneath	Day	Circle	Death	Master	Cosmic

A medley of thinking games

Before we round off this chapter with some story starters, here is a medley of techniques children can use to generate further ideas. A few of the sections below relate specifically to SF, but most can be used with any genre.

What if

This activity combines brainstorming with inference, reasoning and speculation. Put a what-if scenario to the class and add three subsidiary questions –

- What would the world be like?
- What problems could we have?
- How might we solve those problems?

Although here we are using the technique to create ideas for SF stories and to 'build worlds', what-if is more widely used as a problem-solving tool and to generate questions for philosophical discussions. Even when the scenarios are fantastical, the ideas that are explored often relate to real-world issues. See for instance Bowkett, 2015.

Here are some scenarios for the children to discuss –

- What if a large asteroid was discovered heading for Earth? Impact will be in four years' time, and if it hit, nine-tenths of the human race would be destroyed.
- What if the asteroid hit?
- What if slow glass really existed (see page 55)?
- What if you and only you discovered a time portal that would allow you to travel backwards and forwards in time? What if someone else found out about it?
- What if superior aliens arrived on Earth, promising to cure all diseases in humans and end poverty, but only if humans became their slaves?
- What if a small number of humans evolved that were telepathic? They can think together (acting as one mind) and read other people's thoughts.

For many more what-if ideas, try Wikipedia 'list of science fiction themes'.

The Merlin game

Explain to the children that Merlin the wizard is actually our own imagination that can magically transform ideas. So, we can take an idea and –

a)   Make it bigger (enlarge).
b)   Make it smaller (reduce).
c)   Take something away (eliminate).
d)   Put in something extra (add).
e)   Change it round (reverse).
f)   Pull the idea in a different direction (stretch).

So, aliens come to Earth…

a)   At first, we welcome them. They are friendly and helpful. But then more and more of them arrive. Or, the aliens are the size of cats to begin with, but in Earth's atmosphere they grow and grow.

b)   The human population is shrinking (for whatever reason), and when the aliens arrive they say that they can help us to survive. But do we trust them? Or, instead of writing a story about aliens, I could write a haiku poem.

c)   The aliens destroy their superior technology when they come to earth to stop humans from using it to destroy each other. Or, I write the story from the villain's point of view.

d)   Two alien races arrive on Earth, each claiming sanctuary. Or, I can think about a story with alien invasion *and* time travel.

e)   I can tell the story from the alien's point of view. Or, human beings are the aliens when they invade another world.

f)   I can write several stories about the meeting between humans and aliens. Or, humans and aliens can breed together, producing a new type of creature.

Thumbnails

These are short overviews based on novels, short stories, films and comics. Create a bank of them (not just SF) that children can subsequently use as a resource if they're looking for ideas to write about. Often there's enough information in a back cover blurb to allow children to create a thumbnail –

- A person invents a time machine and uses it to see what the future is like.
- Humans discover a strange monolith on the Moon that helps us to evolve.
- Radiation from a huge meteor shower makes most of humanity blind. The same radiation causes a new type of mobile predatory plant to evolve.
- Developments in technology allow cyborgs (half human, half machine) to be created.

Word cloud

Free online software allows the user to upload text and arrange it into a 'vocabulary collage' with control over size, font, colour and other features. Turn this into a useful activity by asking children to contribute words from stories they've written. Or use word cloud posters as colourful displays of genre-related terms children can use subsequently in their writing. See for example https://www.wordclouds.com.

Story starters

Here are some SF story openings that can be used with techniques explained elsewhere in the chapter to help children plot out the whole story.

1.　There was *something* weird about him, that was for sure. He was too calm. Too composed. In his place, Skoot would have been suffering a full sweat knowing that if the General caught up with him, he'd order the troops to fire on sight; immediate execution for being an enemy of the State.

　　'So whatcha called, pilgrim?' She cast a glance at the stranger's eyes and looked away again quickly. Skoot figured she was a good judge of character; had to be in her line of work, on the streets, finding rat-runs for people to escape from the Zone (and sometimes even the planet, as in this case). But *his* face was a closed book; handsome, fresh, 20-something and totally unreadable.

2.   They told me that I would never leave here. They also said that the other children and I were very special, and because of that we would in years to come be able to help the whole human race. At first, when I was very young and they brought me to Genco, I thought it was a school. There were lots of other children here, and we played and we learned. My parents were upset to let me go, but they had been instructed to do it by the Dominus and were honoured to obey even though their hearts were broken. They said that they would come to see me as often as they could, but Deevis, who leads us, said that would not be possible. They wondered why, I remember; and I wondered why. But now I know.

3.   For many thousands of years Earth's people had slept. Each of the planet's ten million surviving inhabitants were sealed safely in the sleep cabinets that protected them from the effects of time and that constantly looked after their every need.

Not one of the sleepers looked a day older than when they had entered the cabinet so many centuries ago; indeed, the hibernation cabinets would ensure that every one of them would remain unchanged forever if need be.

Before the time of the great Resting, wars of unimaginable violence had devastated the planet. Whole continents had been laid to waste and many of the world's species destroyed, even to the depths of the oceans, which had boiled with the heat of the bombs. For 60 years the global superpowers had battled until only scattered fragments of the population remained, many of them crippled or helpless survivors left to die later in the smoke and ruins of the conflict.

4.   High above the Earth's atmosphere, there was a sudden flash of radiation as the Drogon war fleet emerged from hyperspace. A hundred thousand battle craft had travelled halfway across the galaxy to conquer the unsuspecting planet below.

Scans had revealed that there were a number of intelligent species on this world. The most powerful of these were bipeds that stood about ten times taller than the largest Drogon warrior. They had built great cities across the globe. An even cleverer race – four-legged with whiskers and a tail – often shared the bipeds' dwellings and seemed to do nothing but eat and laze around all day. Perhaps they were the true rulers of the world.

'We will conquer them all!' roared Hoggg, Supreme Overlord of the Fleet. He glared at the scanner screens with his six red eyes (one of which was covered over with a patch) and issued his attack plans.

A Drogon ship broke rank and went skimming down towards the Earth's surface.

5.   I loved this little world. I had worked here for over 25 years, gradually growing used to the empty white hills draped in the blackest of shadows; to the endless craters, to the sky that never showed even a hint of blue. Back then, half a lifetime ago, I had travelled here for adventure, perhaps a little danger, perhaps a little romance… I had not found any of it. Instead there was the routine of the job and the iron discipline of doing all the right things to keep yourself alive – especially when much of your time was spent in a pressure suit working beyond the dome. I had grown used to it all and thought I would live out the rest of my days the same way, until I heard about the Moondiamond.

4 Writing a historical story

Summary of the chapter

- Introduction. Definition and characteristics of historical fiction. Touching on the idea that the mysticism in the exemplar story 'The Dreamstones' means it overlaps with fantasy. Mention of alternative histories as a sub-genre of historical fiction.
- Background to the exemplar story. The tale can be found in the chapter on 'Modelling the Writing', page 189.
- Decision-making in writing. Types of comprehension questions and 'interrogating' the text.
- Some tips on research. Using timelines as a research/planning tool.
- Planning a story in terms of age range and therefore language level and story length. Activity: comparing two opening scenes from 'The Dreamstones' written for two different ages of reader.
- Thinking about the time span of a story and further tips on handling time.
- Anachronisms. Using a 'spot the mistakes' image to introduce the idea.
- Point of view/first and third person writing.
- Some tips on writing style. Looking at overwriting. Asking children to look at the story with a critical eye and suggesting ideas for improving it.
- Planning sheet for writing historical fiction.
- Editing and proofreading – some tips and a practice piece.
- Activity: Celtic story grid.
- Story suggestions using characters from 'The Dreamstones'.

Introduction

Historical fiction consists of stories that are based around events that actually happened at a specific time and that feature authentic locations. Both real and invented characters may appear in them. In the same way that science fiction utilises scientific concepts, and so helps to familiarise children with them, encouraging young writers to try historical fiction can lead to a greater under-standing of particular cultures and key figures existing at those times. As such, writing historically based stories can form a useful aspect of any history topic – Ancient Egypt, Ancient Greece, pre-Roman Britain and many others. In this chapter, we touch on a 'history mystery' set around 50 AD as the Romans were pushing northwards through the Midlands of England (for more background, see page 88).

The aspects of a historical story mirror those of other genres –

Plot, consisting of –

- An introduction to the world of the story: setting the time and place.
- Rising tension and action as the problem and its associated dangers become clear.
- The climax of the story.
- The aftermath, as balance and harmony are restored.
- The denouement, where any plot threads are tied up and any further issues are resolved.

Note: Compare this structure with the basic narrative template on page 38.

Characters

The standard advice is that characters based on real people should be faithful to the historical facts and to the legacy of the persons portrayed. Such char-acters should reflect what's known about those people's appearance, beliefs, position in society and other elements of characterisation. Invented characters should similarly act in accordance with what's known about the period when the action takes place.

Setting

Researching historical times and events takes on an extra dimension of mean-ing (and hopefully enjoyment) when it forms part of the planning strategy prior to writing a story. Learning the facts of history goes hand-in-hand with encour-aging children to use their imaginations to visualise what it must have been like to live at a particular time in the past. In the same way that we advise young writers to use all of their senses to imagine a scene they want to write about and to use vivid details when describing it, so those same skills prove valuable when they learn about other times and places. This is similar to the 'world building' necessary to create believable environments in science fiction and fantasy stories (see page 71).

Conflict

Conflict of different kinds between the characters gives a story its energy – its tension, drama and pace. In 'The Dreamstones', conflict arises on a personal level between the protagonist Weland and his rival, Ambior; on a clan level with the arrival of the stranger Carad and the hostility of the priest Ariovis; and on a cultural level between the Celtic tribes and the invading Roman legions. (In a story this short, these are just touched upon but could be used as the basis for a more extended version or a series of linked short stories.)

Theme

This has been explored elsewhere (see for instance page 31). Because themes form the foundation on which all stories are built, those stories set in historical times are likely to mirror important themes in today's world. The themes of cultural beliefs and values, militarism and the will to oppression found in 'The Dreamstones' echo events happening across the planet at present. Introducing and exploring themes through the medium of story helps children to learn more, explore and form opinions about them in reality.

Similarly, researching and writing about a chosen culture helps to deepen children's understanding of those cultures' beliefs and values. So on one level, while the mystical element in 'The Dreamstones' can be used as an example of when genres overlap (for more on this, see page 56), more importantly it creates the opportunity to discuss the **paganism/polytheism** of the Celts and how this compares and contrasts with the children's own spiritual worldview.

So-called 'alternative histories' can bring the same benefits. Here, variations on actual historical events are explored through fiction. So, what if the Roman Empire didn't collapse and the Romans continued to occupy large swathes of Britain for a much longer period? What if the Romans had never come to Britain and its tribal people continued to believe in the gods and in local nature spirits for hundreds of years more?

Thinking about alternative histories blends historical research with inference, speculation and what we might call 'imaginative reach'. One technique for introducing this variation on historical fiction is the 'What if' game on page 79.

Background to the exemplar story 'The Dreamstones'

The story is set around 50 AD in a Celtic settlement that today is called Hallaton, a village lying 16 miles east-southeast of Leicester (which in those times was called Ratae, 'the place of ramparts'). The plot of the story is based on the find in November 2000 of a hoard of thousands of coins, other silver objects and a Roman silver gilt parade helmet, together with further artefacts including numerous leg bones of pigs (97% of all the bones discovered there). Their existence at the shrine remains a mystery. The treasure buried at Hallaton represents enormous wealth and highlights the importance of the site as a religious centre.

Archaeological research has established that the shrine was enclosed by a wooden palisade and polygonal ditch, which separated the sacred space within from the world outside. Pigs and other animals would have been sacrificed there to the various gods the local clans believed in. These included –

Moccus. He was the pig god associated with agricultural fertility, prosperity and also craft and trade.

Taranis, Teutates and Eusos. These are gods' names that relate to 'thunder', 'people' and 'master' and may be different forms of the same male deity.

Epona, a deity from Gaul. She was a horse goddess and is associated with the ritual sacrifice of horses in some British Iron Age sites. To the Celts, the world was 'enchanted', infused by the gods and by local spirits and elementals, and but a thin veil separated the mortal world from the Otherworld where the ancestors dwelt.

At this time the Romans had turned Ratae (Leicester) into a garrison town, capturing it in 44 AD and building a fort there in 48 AD. Some researchers think that prior to this, Ratae was a Celtic settlement. The people of Celtic Ratae and throughout the East Midlands were known as the Corieltauvi. They were largely an agricultural people comprised of a federation of small, self-governing tribal groups.

It is thought that the Corieltauvi offered little resistance to Roman occupation and rule, though for the sake of the story some dramatic licence has been used to suggest that Vepomaros, the village ruler, and his people did not take kindly to Roman interference in their way of life. Similarly, the character of Carad is based on the historical figure of Caratacus (Welsh Caradog), a chieftain of the Catuvellauni tribe, who led the British resistance to the Roman conquest.

Incidentally, many items from the 'Hallaton Hoard' can be found on display at the museum in Market Harborough in Leicestershire.

Decision-making in writing

Creating a piece of writing depends heavily on asking questions and making decisions. An important guiding principle is that everything should happen for a good reason that makes the story work more effectively. One way of developing these core skills in children so that they can apply them to their own work is to help them to 'interrogate the text' of other stories. This involves close and critical reading and the framing of questions focusing on the author's intentions at every level, from plot structure to the choice of individual words. It's important to point out, however, that stories should be read first for enjoyment. In our opinion, a first reading of stories with a critical eye dampens the pleasure the experience can bring. Likewise, we think that children can and should think critically when planning a story and when editing it, but not so much during the writing itself, in order that the creative flow and the enjoyment that brings can be sustained.

An annotated version of 'The Dreamstones' begins on page 190.

The annotations anticipate some of the questions the children might ask about the story. You can use the notes as examples of the kinds of things children might look for or show them the plain version and ask them to come up with questions of their own. Alternatively, show them the following questions and ask the children to think of with some ideas. Numbers at the end of each sentence refer to the paragraphs in the annotated story) –

a) Why do you think the author set the story just before the time of the festival of Samhain (end of October)? (1)

b) Why does the writer bother to mention that Weland's village is called Hallaton now? (1)

c)   What descriptive details of place does the author include in the first few paragraphs of the story?

d)   Why do you think the writer describes Bettrys to some extent, but not Ambior? (4–5)

e)   Why do you think the author makes Carad compare Weland to 'a little hare'?

f)   What do we learn of Weland's personality from his encounter with Carad? (10 and 14)

g)   The writer begins the next scene with Carad finishing the story of his tribe's skirmish with the Romans. Why didn't the author describe Carad's first meeting with Vepomaros and the other people of the village? (16)

h)   Do you think the fact that Carad tells his story only to the men of the village is sexist? If so, do you think the author intended this? Why doesn't the author say 'Vepomaros, Brennus and other people of the settlement listened closely as Carad told his story'? (17)

i)   What impression do we get of Bettrys after Carad has told his tale? (21)

j)   Why does the author leave Ariovis's implied threat 'hanging in the air'? In other words, why doesn't Ariovis come straight out and accuse Carad of actually being Caratacus? (22)

k)   Why do you think Carad uses the metaphors of the wolf and the sheep to urge the villagers to resist the Romans? (23)

l)   Why doesn't the author include dialogue about what the people think of Carad's speech? (24)

m)   Why do you think the author bothers to mention that the moon was 'bright and full'? (26)

n)   Do you think that Bettrys's 'future sight' makes the story less believable or not? Why? (30)

o)   What is superstition? Do you think Bettrys and Weland are just being superstitious? If not, what is the difference between superstition and what Weland and Bettrys are doing? (39)

p)   Why do you think the author mention's Bettrys's hair again? (41)

q)   Why does the author use shorter paragraphs in this part of the story? (46–48)

r)   What age of reader do you think the story is intended for? How have you decided this?

Different kinds of questions can be devised when quizzing the text. As children become more adept at framing these, they will recognise them more easily in comprehension exercises –

- Literal questions where the answers are explicitly stated in the text; for example, *The great festival of Samhain marked the end of summer and the start of long cold winter months.* What did the festival of Samhain mark or represent?
- Cause and effect questions. These often begin with 'why' and require children to read the text carefully to find either the cause or the effect. Example: *Carad's father Brennus had sent him out on to the hills to herd the sheep. As Samhain drew closer and bad weather was due, the animals had to be brought closer to where the people lived. Wolves roamed the countryside and were especially hungry, and therefore bold, in the wintertime.* Why did Brennus send Carad into the hills to round up the sheep?
- Inferential questions. These can be challenging, as the answers are not necessarily stated clearly in the text but may be implied by the writer. They require children to reason their way to a conclusion. Example: *Why do you think the author bothers to mention that the moon was 'bright and full'?* (Paragraph 26. To heighten the atmosphere of celebration and create the reason why Carad could later follow the path towards Ratae without carrying a torch [which could be dangerous, as Roman soldiers would more easily spot him].)
- Opinion questions. More robust answers to these are supported by one or more reasons. Example: *Why do you think the writer describes Bettrys to some extent, but not Ambior?* (Because she is a main character while Ambior is not, and because when we know that Bettrys is pretty we can understand one reason why Carad likes her so much.)
- Vocabulary questions. These ask children to work out the meaning of words based on the context in which they are used. Example: *Using what else you are told in paragraph 42, what do you think the word 'garrison' means?*

Some tips on research

- If you are linking historical story writing to a history topic, be sure to include some details on setting using accurate details, specific figures of the time and cultural details to give children insight into how invented characters would look and behave. Also explore conflicts of the time to help generate ideas for story lines.

- Help children to tease out themes relevant to the period that would give their stories a solid foundation.
- Be on the lookout for vivid details that would give life and colour to the children's stories.
- Ideally, show the class age-appropriate documentaries and dramas of the chosen period. Are there any children's novels, comics or films that they could access to help study the topic? Is a trip to a museum or historical site possible?
- Discuss 'artistic licence' with the class – the notion that this can involve a distortion of facts or contextual inaccuracies to make the story more exciting or accessible for other reasons. Balance this with the idea that when writing historical fiction, distortions of fact should be carefully considered: it's easy to 'tip the balance' so that inaccuracies, if they are spotted, can render the imagined world less believable and/or jolt the reader out of the story. (For instance, when watching a TV drama recently about the Roman invasion of Britain, we laughed aloud when a wanderer came upon two Roman guards on watch and said, 'Hi guys!' In the same drama, one of the characters spoke about 'turning back the hands of time', a metaphor referring to the hands on a clock face: such clocks did not exist in Roman times. These instances may be intentional, to appeal to a modern audience perhaps, or maybe they were written into the script in ignorance. While many children might not pick up on errors like these – especially in the age of digital timepieces – they should at least be aware that mention of modern technology or idioms weakens a historical story.) Also see 'Anachronisms' on page 99.
- Emphasise that children should consider putting in just enough historical background and detail to make the world of the story come alive. Too much information slows down the action and dampens the tension and excitement of the tale.
- Timelines. These are useful for recording researched information, so giving children a 'broad sweep' of understanding related to a chosen historical period. The visual shows a conventional layout. The timeline is a flexible visual tool that can be applied to events in one or more characters' lives and can be used as a way of helping children to understand and control the time span of a story.

Timeline:

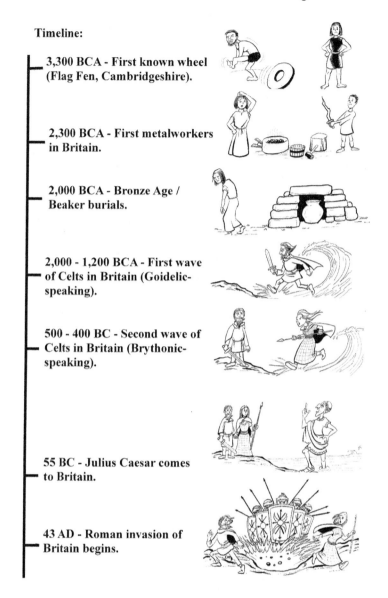

3,300 BCA - First known wheel (Flag Fen, Cambridgeshire).

2,300 BCA - First metalworkers in Britain.

2,000 BCA - Bronze Age / Beaker burials.

2,000 - 1,200 BCA - First wave of Celts in Britain (Goidelic-speaking).

500 - 400 BC - Second wave of Celts in Britain (Brythonic-speaking).

55 BC - Julius Caesar comes to Britain.

43 AD - Roman invasion of Britain begins.

Take it further

Timelines can be created by individual children when researching their own stories. However, if all the children are writing about the same historical period, the whole class can be involved in making a colourful and vibrant timeline display.

Age range, language level and story length

These matters may not arise, given that most children write stories for people of their own age. Also, they will be constrained by the vocabulary they currently possess and perhaps by the limited writing time they have, whether in school and/or at home.

However, deciding on the age range of the reader and what follows from that is a useful skill for a writer to possess, if only at this point as an analytical tool in assessing texts the children read.

'The Dreamstones' is intended for children around Y4–5 (though we appreciate that the reading age in those years will vary widely). Various outcomes at the planning stage were made as a result of that early decision –

- Sentences and paragraphs would be relatively short.
- Historical details would be given a light touch, enough hopefully to evoke an impression of the time and place but not so much that readers become distracted and bored.
- Language would be simpler rather than more sophisticated. Terms that children may not know, such as 'shrine' and 'sacrifice', are explained in other words.
- Violence is kept to a minimum. The aim is to make the different conflicts within the story believable, because they are serious, without allowing mention of violent acts to become gratuitous or inappropriate. Blood didn't appear once!

Tip This point raises the notion of gratuitous violence in stories. In our experience, boys especially enjoy reading and writing about blood and gore. That's fine as far as it goes, but if the work is to be read by others, it is one of the author's responsibilities to ensure that the level of violence serves a purpose in supporting the narrative and is appropriate for the intended audience.

- The 'love relationship' likewise is suggested in the story and by the end of the tale has taken a step closer to fruition. Weland is 13, and presumably Bettrys would be the same age. Both might have sex on their minds, but it's the *age of the reader* that is important in deciding how the relationship should be portrayed.

Activity

Two versions of 'The Dreamstones' exist, the one in this book and another that was written for older readers. Show the following extracts from both to the class and ask the children to point of the differences in terms of language level, sentence structure, amount of detail etc.

1.   The tribe had been getting ready for the celebration for days. It was the great festival of Samhain. It marked the end of summer and the start of long cold winter months. The people of the tribe – the Corieltauvi – dwelt in a small settlement in a narrow valley. One day this place would be called Hallaton. It was where a boy named Weland and his family lived.

   Weland was thirteen years old. His father Brennus had sent him out on to the hills to herd the sheep. As Samhain drew closer and bad weather was due, the animals had to be brought closer to where the people lived. Wolves roamed the countryside and were especially hungry, and therefore bold, in the wintertime.

   The pigs, sheep and cattle that would not be used for breeding were sacrificed to the gods. This happened at a special shrine or sacred place that had been built on the hill. A wooden fence partly circled the shrine. In the very centre was a great block of wood. Here the animals were killed as offerings. But people also left little statues, coins and other gifts too.

2.   The doorway was opening to the dark time of the year. Even though the sun shone and there was still some warmth in the wind, I could feel the first bite of winter in my blood. I had never liked the snows and the endless nights, but Bettrys the daughter of the wise-man Cunor had made me listen with my soul rather than my imagination. And yes, beyond the months of the Ice Moon I could hear the whisperings of new beginnings and the stirring of the seed below ground. She was right, as in so many ways: the ancient gods would look after us even though the shadows gathered around us and the light burned low.

   I had been given the task of bringing sheep down off the hills. The cattle and pigs were already penned and the harvests gathered up in the granary and storage pits. Soon the animals that were not chosen as breeding stock would be slaughtered and the meat salted so that it would keep until Spring, save what had been prepared for the great celebration of Summer's End. Even here on the ridge I could smell the sweet smoke of the fires from the spits, and, beneath, the boiling pots where the pigs' carcasses would be scalded and scraped ready for the feast. The eating tonight, and for the following two nights of the year's turning, would be fine indeed!

Time span

Advise children during the planning stage to think about how much time passes in the world of their story between the opening and closing scenes. The action in 'The Dreamstones' for instance takes place within 24 hours. Having a sense of time helps young writers to steer the narrative more surely and avoid errors relating to when in the day, week, month etc. particular events occur. It's easy to become confused and lose track if the passage of time has not been considered. This leads to inconsistencies creeping in. Once decisions about time span have been made, research can be carried out more effectively. Knowing that Carad's arrival at Weland's village occurs at the end of October gives insight into what the weather will be like, what the landscape will look like, what will be happening with regard to crops and livestock, what clothes the characters will be wearing and so on.

Time span can be built into the story line planning tool we looked at on page 9 and might help children to have further ideas to make their stories more colourful and dramatic. Setting a story during a summer heatwave, for example, might spark the idea of characters running out of water as they trek across an arid landscape, or create the opportunity to describe a spectacular thunderstorm when the weather breaks.

A further factor related to time span is checking that events are consistent with each other in terms of when they happen. For instance, when Weland realises that Ambior is leading the Roman horsemen to the settlement to capture Carad and his men, he knows he has time to get there first by going through the woods. If he had been closer to Ratae when he encountered Ambior, this would not have been possible. Having a sense of time passing when writing the story allows this mistake to be avoided and also creates the dramatic device of a time limit to boost the tension.

More tips on handling time

- Backstory. This is a history or background to a character, place or event that leads up to the main plot. In a short tale, a backstory would necessarily be brief. For instance, by way of introducing the fact that the Romans have established a garrison not far from Carad's village, we could say something like – 'The Romans first came to Britain nearly a century before with Julius Caesar's two invasions. These were only partly successful. Then in 43 AD a more powerful army led by general Aulus Plautius arrived and forged north, encountering Carad's people several years later'.
- Flashback. This is a reference or scene within a text that takes the reader to some point in the past within the world of the story. For example, we could say – 'As Carad scanned the hillsides for sheep he remembered when, as a very young child, he had first been brought out here by his father, Brennus'.
- Foreshadowing. This gives the reader a hint of something that will happen in the future in the world of the story. Bettrys's gift of 'future sight' is the plot device used to anticipate the arrival of Roman soldiers at the village later that night, while Carad, just before he leaves, anticipates a time when the Romans are gone from the land (though this goes beyond the time span of the story).

All of these narrative techniques require what might be called a leap of the imagination through time, in the same way that writing in the third person requires imaginative manipulation of space (more on this below). Some children tell their stories as it were in 'linear real time'; the character did this and then, and then, and then… In other words, their stories move in a straight line from beginning through to the end. This is not in itself a bad thing – indeed, 'The Dreamstones' is a straightforward linear tale. But when children become more familiar with the techniques explained above, they can tackle their creative writing projects with greater versatility.

Activity

Once the children have read or listened to 'The Dreamstones', show them this visual as you explain backstory, flashback and foreshadowing.

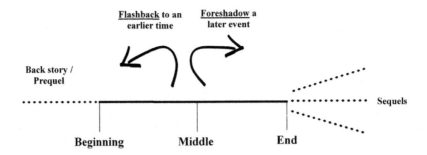

Ask the children to think of examples that the author might have included in the story. For instance –

- Backstory. How the Romans first came to Britain/A scenario of Celtic tribes warring with each other/How people first established the settlement where Weland lives.
- Flashback. Brennus recalling the time when he was first sent out alone to bring in the sheep/Details of how Bettrys first gained future sight/Weland remembering Ariovis's bullying from years before.
- Foreshadowing. Here you can use the examples of Bettrys's future sight and Carad's anticipation of the Romans leaving Britain.

At this point you might also talk about –

- Prequels. These are stories of events that take place before the action of the present tale. In the context of 'The Dreamstones', prequels could include the spread of the Roman influence northwards from the south coast/The story of the cavalryman who was unhorsed by Weland/The tale of how Bettrys was tutored to develop her gift of future sight.
- Sequels. These are tales that continue or expand upon the present story. Examples might be Carad's journey to and encounter with Cartimandua of the Brigantes tribe and what follows from that meeting/A soldier's account of the pursuit of Carad northwards/What happens to Weland and Bettrys when they are grown up (they may for instance become involved in the uprising against the Romans led by Boudicca around 60 AD).
- Parallel stories. Stories using the same backdrop of events as the present tale but featuring or told from the viewpoint of other characters. As a writing project, you can suggest to children that they write Bettrys's story, or Carad's, or Vepomaros's etc.

Anachronisms

An anachronism is something that is out of its proper time (though the Greek roots *anakhronismos* – from *ana*, 'backwards', and *khronos*, 'time' – don't make this entirely clear).

When writing historically based stories, children must be careful not to introduce things that could not have existed at the time. Most obviously this would include recent technology, but more subtly modern idioms – see page 92. If children have only recently been introduced to the idea of anachronisms or don't have a firm grasp of the concept, our advice would be to let them go ahead and write their story anyway and check for anachronisms afterwards, using the exercise as an opportunity to sharpen their analytical/editing skills. This strategy only becomes an issue if the plot relies heavily on something that could not have existed at the time, such as a Celtic tribe defeating a Roman attack by using a minigun!

The illustration features ten anachronisms. How many can the children spot? They are: Union Jack, chimney, vacuum cleaner, camel, gun, wristwatch, trainers, matches, glass window panes and cutlass.

The camel here is something of an odd-one-out, insofar as camels did exist in Celtic times but as far as we know were not brought as far north as Britain. Credit is due to any child who points this out. You can suggest in that case the camel could instead be called an anomaly (from the Greek from *an-*, 'not', and *homalos*, 'even').

Take it further by asking children to come up with sentences featuring anachronisms based on a history topic they have studied.

Point of view

'The Dreamstones' is written in the third person, but the narrative stays with Weland throughout. This has been called 'the parrot on the shoulder' technique, because the reader is like a parrot sitting on Weland's shoulder, forced to experience only what he does. It is, therefore, a limited kind of third person writing.

A more open and flexible way of using the third person is for the author to 'float' above the world of the story, controlling the narrative by switching from character to character. To do this requires an imaginative leap through space, and perhaps time, in the world of the story.

Activity

Play the 'Meanwhile game' to familiarise children with the idea of third person overview. Show the class the visual and annotate it as you go along. Begin at the centre of the concentric circles. You could use any character from the story, but we'll take Weland as our example, standing in the centre.

N

W   E

S

Weland roamed the hillside looking for sheep

Now begin to move outward a step at a time, inviting the children to come up with ideas. You may need to move beyond the events of the story at this point, creating the opportunity for children to research their replies rather than answering immediately.

Weland roamed the hillside looking for sheep. Meanwhile, two miles away in his village...? (Brennus was mending his longbow.)

And while Brennus was mending his longbow, five miles to the west...? (Carad and his men were arriving in the valley.)

And while Carad and his men were arriving in the valley, ten miles to the north...? (Roman soldiers were on patrol around Ratae.)

And so on. In this case you can build actual geographical and historical facts into the game. The primary aim, however, is to help children exercise their imaginations by creating a widening overview of the world in which the story takes place.

Activity

A similar activity is the 'Because game'. This helps children to create reasons for the events or scenarios they imagine. Before you start, discourage any tendency to come up with inappropriate or frivolous ideas. This is important: the game is a variation of the brainstorming technique, and some children may be tempted to call out the first thought that comes into their heads. It's likely that most of the children will have ideas and want to be involved, but to keep the game simple, pick just one idea before moving on. So –

Teacher:	Weland was roaming the hillside because...?
Pupil:	Because he was searching for sheep.
Teacher:	And he was searching for sheep because...?
Pupil:	His father Brennus asked him to.
Teacher:	And Brennus asked him to because...?
Pupil:	He needed all of the sheep to be safe in the village.
Teacher:	And the sheep needed to be safe because...?
Pupil:	Wolves would be a danger.

Teacher: And the wolves would be a danger because…?

Pupil: Winter was coming and there would not be so much food around, so the wolves would be hungry.

Notice that up to this point the children are recalling facts from the story and are beginning to use inference to frame their responses. But now you will need to think on your toes. It makes no sense to ask: 'And winter was coming because…?' unless you are hoping a child answers: 'Because of the Earth's orbit around the sun'. In this case, the 'thought chain' moves away from the story and into the topic of celestial mechanics.

So you might change tack by saying –

Teacher: And during winter people from different tribes became more warlike because…?

Or: During the winter the Romans attacked villages more often because…?

While factually these statements might not be true, the purpose of the game is to develop children's creativity and ability to construct robust reasons.

The 'Because game' can also be used to brainstorm story plots from scratch. Choose a genre and launch the activity with a simple statement –

Teacher: Fantasy story. A boy was running through the woods because…?

Pupil: He was being chased by a wizard.

Teacher: And he was being chased by a wizard because…?

Pupil: The boy had stolen a magical amulet.

Teacher: And he had stolen the magical amulet because…?

Pupil: He needed to pass through the forbidden portal.

Teacher: And the boy wanted to pass through the portal because…?

Plots that evolve by this technique tend to be robust and not arbitrary by virtue of the fact that the chain of ideas is supported by a reason at each point. You can extend the game by going back over the points that have been made and asking for alternatives. So instead of a wizard chasing the boy, it was a dragon – and the dragon was chasing him because…? Also, if any of the reasons linking the ideas prove to be weak, ask the children to come up with other, stronger reasons.

Overwriting

This is the tendency in writing to try too hard to get a point across or describe a character, setting or event by –

- Using too many 'strong' adjectives and verbs.
- Attaching adverbs to every verb.
- Using too many superlatives.
- Tagging dialogue differently each time (said, intoned, exclaimed, yelled etc.).
- Using overblown language and long and often obscure words.
- Exaggerating, which may involve some or all of the above.

Overwritten scenes can quickly bore the reader and weaken rather than strengthen the impact of a story. The rules of thumb with any creative writing are –

- Less is more. Say just enough to make the point and let the reader's imagination fill in the details.
- Use simpler and more familiar words rather than longer, fancier ones. Never use words whose meaning you aren't sure about.
- Don't let sentences and paragraphs become too long.
- Don't struggle to think of fresh similes and metaphors.
- Stick to the point – don't go rambling off on a tangent.
- Use 'said' most of the time when tagging dialogue (telling the reader who said what), changing the tag sometimes if necessary.
- Never try to show off in your writing.

Activity

Here are some examples of overwriting. Ask the children to apply the guidelines above and tone down these scenes (you may need to help some children with the vocabulary!).

a)   After a short while Weland stopped to listen for the bleating of any nearby sheep, holding his breath and becoming as still as stone as his sea green eyes relentlessly scanned the rolling hillsides. High above, clouds surged through the sky on a hurricane-like wind, while buzzards circled ominously as though waiting for some poor creature to die so that they could pounce and tear the animal's flesh asunder with their razor sharp beaks and deadly talons.

Suddenly Weland heard the thunderous drumming of horses' hooves approaching swiftly and then the evil, guttural, menacing, terrifying sound of men's voices. The blood froze in Weland's veins; his heart trembled like a leaf in the middle of a maelstrom and his eyes nearly popped out of his head with terror.

b)   'The Roman hoards could not surround us because we had taken our stand on the hill. Our own men furiously shook their weapons and roared like rampaging bulls at the enemy who, because they knew that our hearts were as strong as oak, cowered back like mice upon glimpsing the cat about to leap. Thick woodland lay behind us and deadly marshland with its scummy, stagnant stinking waters spread out in front, creating an impenetrable obstacle that would thwart the Romans' fierce desire to obliterate us. My spirit soared high like the eagle and I felt as though I were one with the gods. My blood sped through my veins swifter than an arrow flashes through the air as my voice reached a new crescendo of rage. 'Victory!' I yelled stentoriously. 'May your bodies writhe in a thousand agonies before you die, and then your corpses rot in the earth and be consumed by myriads of maggots. May your disembodied souls wander lost among innumerable hells, plagued by horrifying demons, tortured by the vicissitudes of your plight. And may you be forgotten as swiftly as opalescent mist vanishes under the sparkling and scintillant rays of the morning's first sunlight!'

c)   A powerful blow strong enough to fell a giant smashed excruciatingly into the side of Weland's head and slammed him instantaneously to the ground.

'You are not even fit to herd sheep', boomed a familiar voice tauntingly. Ambior's clawed hands clenched Weland's arms in a vice-like grip and hauled him up as easily as if he were made of twigs and rags – only to pummel and batter him down again, such that Weland's body was smashed back with fearsome force into the dirt.

But then hatred born of many years of such humiliations smouldered and then exploded like an erupting volcano in Weland's chest. Rage burst through him, and this gave him almost superhuman strength. Quicker than lightning he leaped up and delivered a devastating punch to Ambior's face. The larger boy looked momentarily surprised before his eyes closed and he crumpled like a rag doll at Weland's feet.

Editing and proofreading

Children should be encouraged to look through their work once the writing is done. They are likely to spot more errors and have more ideas for beneficial changes if they come back to the work after a 'cooling off' period of a day or so. Trying to edit and correct while writing the first draft inhibits the creative flow and makes for a frustrating writing experience.

Encourage children to ask two useful questions as they review their work with a more critical eye –

- What changes can I make so that this is the best I can do today?
- What have I learned by writing this that will help to make my next piece of writing even better?

The first question acknowledges that children are still learning (as indeed are adult authors), and that a writer's best work at that stage of her development arises as a result of reflection, changes of mind and polishing and refining a first attempt. The second question reinforces the first, encouraging children to look at their work in a more analytical way, to clarify techniques and working principles that hopefully they can incorporate into subsequent pieces. By all means, help and guide children along this road, but allow them some independence as they make up their own minds about how to improve their work.

Although the terms editing and proofreading are often used interchangeably, there is an important difference. Editing tends to focus on the general structure of the work, in the case of stories how the plot unfolds, how characters develop and how pace, tension and atmosphere are controlled. Proofreading attends to more superficial issues such as spelling, punctuation and grammar; a kind of final tweaking and polishing before the writer moves on to the next project.

Incidentally, the 'proof' in proofreading means to confirm or test something, in this case the robustness and accuracy of the writing. The same sense of the word crops up in the term 'the exception that proves the rule'. This sounds like a contradiction at first glance, but in fact refers to the idea that the exception tests the rule to see if it still applies.

Below is an extract from 'The Dreamstones' (paragraphs 45–49) containing ten errors. Invite the children to spot these, relying either on their knowledge of spelling etc., or by comparing the extract with the corresponding paragraphs in the full story (page 190).

Take it further

● Ask children to deliberately put errors in their work for classmates to spot.

Tip These can be based on aspects of spelling etc. that you want to revise with the class, or on an aspect of writing that you've just introduced and want the children to practise.

● Encourage children to annotate their work sometimes, rather than redraft. This can be more engaging than asking children to undertake what many perceive as 'writing it all out again'.
● When you come across a typo or inconsistency in a book you're reading (including this one!), show the page to the class and ask if any of the children can spot the errors. (This implicitly sends home the message that even professionally written, edited and proofread texts are rarely perfect – some errors usually slip through the net.)

Weland continued moving at a brisk pace, seeing his way by moonlight. Is eyes grew used to the silvery landscape as he gazed down into the valley. His attention was fixed there, so it was that he failed to notice what was write in front of him until it was two late.

A powerful blow struck the side of his head and smashed him to the ground. 'You're not even fit to herd sheep', said a familiar voice. Ambior's strong hands grabbed Welland's tunic and dragged him up, only to batter him down again with two more mighty punches.

As Weland lay dazed he heard the heavy clumping of horses' and was aware of two or three cavalrymen riding past. Ambior was already returning to the settlement with the Romans. Weland had failed in his mission. *Although*, he thought, *I could still get there ahead of them by going through the woods. If only...*

Ambior started to haul Weland to his feet fore a third time. But Weland was expecting this and swung a solid right fist into Ambior's face. Weland thought he would need to fight hard for victory, but with a soft grunt Ambior simply fell and lay still, quiet unconscious.

Weland chuckled as he realised why – he still held the dreamstone in his hand and it had added wait to his blow.

For a moment he thought his troubles were over, but then to his dismay he saw one of the roman horsemen turn and begin cantering back. The soldier drew his short stabbing sword as he came.

Looking for improvements

Leonardo da Vinci allegedly said that art is never finished, only abandoned. While editing work to clear up errors and think about improvements is important, true experience in writing is gained by moving on to other more diverse and hopefully more challenging projects.

Many writers, having completed a story or poem leave it for a while to 'cool off' and come back to it some time later so that it can be looked at again with fresh eyes. When the work is going well, a writer is immersed in the world of the story such that trying to edit or analyse at the same time can interrupt the creative flow. Our advice is to encourage children, once they've planned their work, simply to enjoy writing it and not to worry at that stage about trying to get it just right. In our opinion, this guideline even includes not worrying about correct spelling or punctuation. These are important of course, but errors can be tidied up later rather than during the primary act of trying to translate what's in one's mind's eye into words on the page or screen.

With this in mind, 'free writing' is a widely used technique. Here, a writer simply launches into a story and just lets the images and words flow without any attempt to make corrections during the process and ideally without stopping. Free writing can take place when some planning has been done, or with just a few details in mind. The author Douglas Hill would sometimes use just a single idea as a springboard for free writing, simply letting ideas stream out onto the screen. The principle here is 'how do I know what I think until I see what I've written?'

Free writing is similar to stream-of-consciousness writing. This is an unstructured and unedited flow of ideas, written as they come to mind without being consciously considered, just noticed (as such, the technique could also be called stream-of-subconsciousness writing). To try this activity with the children –

● Choose a character and write a description of the entire person, including some background. It's not essential to have picked a genre first. Just a name will do. Here are some character faces you can use, or select from else- where, or just make one up.

● Don't try and remember rules of grammar, punctuation or spelling. The aim is to get the words out on the page as they pop into mind. If the flow of ideas seems to be slowing down, just brainstorm any associations of what you've just written – banana, yellow, peel, skin, slip, cereal, breakfast, milk, cows, grass, fields, countryside, weather, climate, autumn, colours…

- Once the flow of ideas stops, put the work away and leave it for a while. Come back to it later to correct as necessary, give the material further structure and use it to plan a more formalised finished piece.

Using a character as the basis for this kind of writing works well when introducing the technique. With practice, children will be able to use the technique to focus on setting and plot. Stream of consciousness writing can also help to dispel the 'fear of the blank page' and because the focus is on free flow rather than remembering rules, many so-called reluctant writers can be tempted to try it out, thereby gaining in confidence.

When you advise children to keep their work and look back at it some months later, many will realise that they could 'do it better now'. Point out that this means they have learned more about writing well and have gained in experience. It's not necessary or even desirable to rewrite the stories – move on to something new – although old manuscripts can be annotated with the children's ideas for improvement.

Activity

Once you've read 'The Dreamstones' with your class, ask the children if they can see any ways of improving it. When we looked back, there were a number of things we would now do differently –

- A few descriptive details of Weland and some other characters.

Note: The character faces on page 108 can be used for this activity. Ask children to decide which faces match which characters in the story, then add some further details with that specifically in mind.

- More 'multisensory' details of the village and the feasting that went on after Carad arrived.
- More description of the Roman soldiers, to enhance the sense of the threat they pose.
- Extending the encounter between Weland and the Roman horseman to heighten the drama.

● Having Carad explain why he is visiting the tribal leader Cartimandua in particular, and also attaching some risk to this mission insofar as she might side with the Romans.

Story planner

We've looked at a number of techniques for helping children to plan their work; the template below also allows young writers to gather their thoughts. Note that some of the boxes might be completed in parallel with children writing their first draft. The template can easily be adapted to suit other genres.

Story Planner

Title:

Setting:
Historical Period -   Location -
Important events of the time -
Key people of the time -
Any further interesting details of the time -

Key Characters in the Story - Name, Physical Description, Personality:
1)
2)
3)
4)

Theme(s):

Main Problem:

Key Events in the Story:

Story grid

Notes on using a story grid can be found on page 50. The grid can be used in conjunction with the plot ideas below and the story planner.

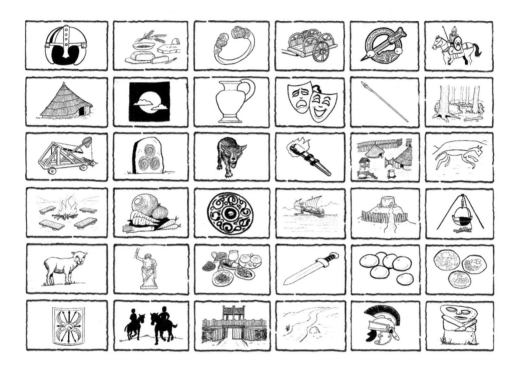

Take it further

● If you use the grid before reading the story to the class, ask for first impressions. What do the children think life was like for Celtic people living 2000 years ago? How would people's lives be different from our own?

Tip You can link this with the idea of anachronisms (see page 99).

● Again, if the children haven't heard the story, offer questions about the grid for them to research, and/or invite children to come up with their own questions. Highlight the notion that asking questions is not to be regarded as an admission of ignorance but rather a sign of healthy curiosity and a desire to find out more. For instance –

- What could object 5/1 be?
- What might be the purpose of having a fire out in the open surrounded by benches – 1/4?
- Why has a fence been built around the hill – 5/3?
- Why are there three pictures of food?
- What does the statue 6/1 represent?
- Why is the statue 2/2 holding a lightning bolt?
- What could the designs on the stone 2/4 mean?
- Why has a picture of a horse been carved into the land – 6/4 – and why doesn't it look much like a horse?

● Encourage children to think **metaphorically** by considering that some of the images could represent more general or abstract ideas. A shield could represent defence. A weapon could stand for conflict or power. A stockade around the village could symbolise a sense of identity and the wish to preserve it. The ship could represent the spirit of adventure.

● Ask children to select two images from the grid, either deliberately or using dice rolls, and create a sentence in which the names of both items appear.

● Split the class into small groups. Give out copies of the grid (enlarged to A3 is ideal) and ask children to cut out images and arrange them along a narrative line (page 9) to create a visual story plan. Groups can add further pictures that they've drawn themselves.

● Place vocabulary related to the Roman invasion of Britain around the grid, some of it to be used by the children as they construct their stories.

● Ask groups to replace certain items on the grid with others they find by researching the topic of the Romans in Celtic Britain.

● Children can create their own story grids for other genres (including their favourite stories in films, comics or text). If you run it as a class activity, be sure that the children are familiar with the motifs and conventions of the chosen genre (see page 30). Ask each child to find or draw two pictures, or come up with two words, related to the genre (two, so that if a child has the same idea as a classmate, she can use her other choice). The grid can be created digitally by typing words and importing pictures into a 6x6 grid blank. Alternatively, groups can build their grids on paper, which can later be photocopied and shared for other groups to try out.

Story ideas based on 'The Dreamstones'

1. Weland travels north with Carad and his men to try and forge an allegiance with Cartimandua of the Brigantes tribe. A) They succeed; B) They fail – what further stories could come out of these scenarios?

2. Ariovis tells the Roman general at Ratae about Bettrys's future sight and conspires to have her kidnapped. Weland finds Carad, and together they set out to rescue her.

3. Bettrys becomes a powerful seer and aids Boudicca in her uprising against the Romans.

4. Romans attack Weland's settlement in the middle of winter. The villagers flee. This story will be a series of **vignettes** following the fate of some of them as they try to survive in the bleak landscape.

5. Warring clans, including Weland's, join forces to fight the Roman advance northwards.

5 Writing a pirate story

Summary of the chapter

- Introduction. Touching on the popularity of pirate adventures and their use as vehicles for increasing children's knowledge of various aspects of narrative fiction. Using pirate adventures as an adjunct to exploring the broader genre of historical fiction. Contextualising pirate adventures as taking place in the Caribbean between the 1660s and 1830s.
- Tropes (recurring motifs or themes) in pirate adventures. How some of these can be used in other genres: space pirates, fantasy world pirates etc.
- Story grid. A visual planner for generating plot ideas. Asking children to interpret and select images to combine with the storyline visual planner.
- Pirates and stereotypes.
- Looking at character motivation – why become a pirate? Linking this with the strength of reasons for action and the believability of the plot.
- Minor characters – assembling a crew.
- Then and now. A research activity highlighting some differences between the world during our 'pirate timeline' and the modern day.
- Vocabulary, anachronisms and the plasticity of language.
- Romanticising. Touching on the idea of glamorising pirates in fiction; making their adventures more colourful, exciting and appealing than they really were.
- Treasure map and riddles. Using these common motifs in pirate adventures. Looking at different kinds of riddles and encouraging children to write their own.

Introduction

We have included pirate stories in this book because we hope that many children will enjoy plotting and writing swashbuckling[1] adventures. And while these stories will be works of fiction, preparing for them can involve researching real people, places and times. More broadly, as we've stated elsewhere, creating pirate stories (and tales from other genres) develops the raft of thinking and communication skills that will benefit children in their writing and speaking more generally.

Pirates seem to be particularly popular with children now. There are pirate films, pirate toys, pirate rides and even pirate-themed parties. There were, of course, actual historical pirates – who were probably not the type of people you would want organising your children's party – but they have been superseded in the popular imagination by the pirate archetypes of the media. The tropes of pirate adventures (walking the plank, searching for buried treasure, pitched sea battles) are as familiar to us now as they probably were rare at the time. This doesn't stop them being great fun! As they are so familiar, they can be a great aid in developing a narrative.

Tropes in pirate stories

Tropes are recurring motifs or themes that help to define, describe and enrich the genre. They contribute to the conventions of a genre; that is, they include the people, places and objects that are conventionally used within a given kind of story.

Tropes in pirate adventures include –

- Talking like a pirate, often with an accent from the West Country and using plenty of nautical slang.
- Wearing earrings, lots of colourful clothes and a tricorn hat.
- Sporting a parrot on the shoulder.
- Having a wooden leg, an eye patch and a hook for a hand.
- Making people who've wronged you walk the plank.
- Studying maps to look for buried treasure.
- Displaying a skull and crossbones or 'Jolly Roger' flag. (In reality, showing the Jolly Roger meant that the pirates were prepared to take prisoners, whereas a blood-red flag signified 'death to all'.)
- Fighting with a flintlock and cutlass.

The tropes of pirates are so familiar that they can even be transplanted, so why not have space pirates plundering the galaxy –

Or sky pirates raiding from giant airships –

Or ice pirates gliding over frozen lakes on distant planets, or sand pirates skimming across barren deserts on sleek land yachts?

Activity

It can be fun adapting pirate lore to a new environment; instead of walking the plank, space pirates threaten their enemies with being shot out into space, sky pirates might use harpoons and grapple guns to try and bring down their enemies' ships. There is endless flexibility.

Showing children a story grid helps them to become familiar with the tropes and conventions of a given genre. See page 50 for notes on how to use the grid to generate ideas and link them to form a plot.

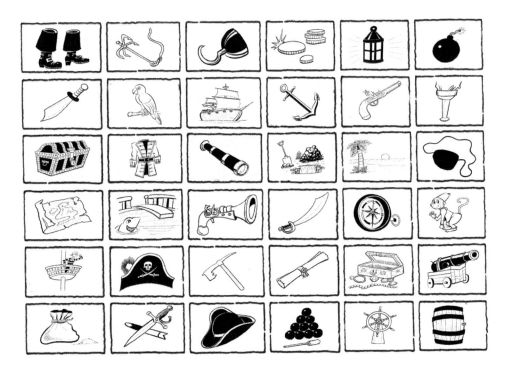

Take it further

- What first impressions can the children deduce about pirates or 'the pirate life' by glancing at the grid as a whole? (For example, pirates were keen to gain treasure; they lived a violent life; they wanted to frighten their opponents.)
- Images from the grid can be cut out and placed along a story line as an aid to organising ideas in a narrative sequence. Also, children can draw their own images or write on scraps of paper to increase the range of ideas they can incorporate into a story. Which images from the grid would the children choose to add detail to the items along a storyline? For instance, for 'conflict' they might pick some of the weapons and also items like the hook, the wooden leg and the eye-patch as representing the consequences of a violent exchange. What other images, ones not featured on the grid, would children choose to accompany the items on the storyline?

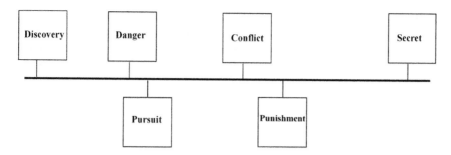

Note: The items on the example story line are 'artfully vague'. That is to say, they offer some information but are general enough to be interpreted in various ways. So we learn that some kind of secret occurs towards the end of the narrative, but different children will probably have different ideas about what that secret might be.

Artful vagueness, plus in this case the positioning of examples along the story line, is a useful technique because it adheres to the creative principle of flexibility within a structure. Children have definite pieces of information to work with but can feel a sense of satisfaction and ownership when they create more details around each.

> **Tip** Playing the counter flip game (page 34) at this point can also help children to generate further ideas.

- Ask the class which tropes can be changed to fit in with different genres – science fiction or fantasy, for example? So the pirate ship could become a spaceship, the cutlass could become a laser-blade, the hook could become a mechanical hand…
- Inference and research. Can the children work out why a crow's nest (1/2) and a tricorn hat (3/1) are so named? What is the origin of words such as cutlass, compass, anchor, blunderbuss (3/3) and keg?
- Speculation. This is also called 'maybe thinking'. Point out the scroll (4/2) and ask what it might be/what may be written on it – possibly a map, a royal pardon, a commission as privateer (a person or ship that is commissioned by the government to engage in war), a personal message, a curse, a riddle, some instructions, a threat, a poem.

Take it further

Try 'if-then' thinking. So for example, if the scroll was a royal pardon, then what has happened that led up to this? Or if the scroll contained instructions, then what might these be and what consequences might follow? Or if the scroll was a curse, then who created the curse and why?

- Thinking metaphorically. We can think of the bomb (6/6) in a literal sense, but it could also represent 'an explosive situation', the idea of 'dropping a bombshell', to have a 'short fuse' or to 'blow a fuse' (i.e. explode with anger). Such phrases are also known as idioms (from the Greek 'to make one's own'); metaphorical expressions that are peculiar to a language. Can the children think of or find out about idioms based on: boot, lamp/light, lookout, anchor, keg, ship, dig/bury, sword?

> **Tip** https://www.thefreedictionary.com/ is a useful resource. Click on the 'Idioms' tab for plenty of ideas.

Pirate stereotypes

Originally 'stereotype' referred to a method of printing from a metal plate, such that many identical copies could be created. Over time, the word came to mean something that conformed to a fixed or general pattern. It's tempting to use character stereotypes in stories because many readers are already familiar with them, thus they represent a kind of 'shorthand' – we only have to mention Captain Hook for a detailed picture to pop into mind. It's OK for children to use character stereotypes if that helps them to engage with the task of writing. However, continued use can lead to lazy thinking, so as children develop their writing skills and become more confident, they should be encouraged to break the stereotype habit and put some effort into creating more original characters (see page 45).

Pirates are usually cast in three modes, the brute, the hero and the rogue.

The brute is the traditional pirate stereotype: huge, violent, bloodthirsty and out for plunder or revenge. Of course, it's fun to tinker with this a little bit, such as making your bloodthirsty pirate have a soft spot for his pet parrot or write poetry in his spare time. He (or she; there were female pirates too) mainly functions as a villain.

The hero is the noble pirate, no less brave but having a clear moral code. Often these characters seem so principled you wonder why they became pirates in the first place (see 'Motivation' below).

The rogue is halfway between the two, being a charming charismatic schemer who you are never sure whether you can trust or not. This character might have a moral code, but if so, they keep it to themselves. Will they betray you? Will they turn up trumps in the end? Who knows?

Activity

● What changes could be made to make these characters a little more original and individual? See the Merlin technique on page 80.
● Repeat the activity for stereotypical tropes found in the story grid on page 118. How could we change the parrot on the shoulder trope to make it more original? Maybe the captain has trained it to take messages, which it speaks on arrival. Or perhaps it has a highly developed homing sense and can always advise the captain which way to go to reach a safe haven. How could we change the galleon, the plank, the anchor etc.?

Motivation

Why choose to be a pirate? The brute obviously (but not always) for riches, power and a chance for a good rampage, but what about the hero or the rogue?

Brainstorming possible reasons that someone might end up as a captain of a pirate ship can be a fun starting point and help to shape the character. Here are just a few –

- Unjustly accused of a crime, so they can never go home until they clear their name.
- Searching for a life of excitement or freedom impossible anywhere else.
- Searching for a lost love captured by other pirates.
- Captured themselves but then took over the ship by outwitting or outfighting the previous captain.
- Sentenced to the gallows for a minor crime only to escape and dedicate themselves to ridding the seas of their enemies.
- Employed by the crown to raid enemy ships.
- In possession of a map showing the location of fabulous wealth – acquired by dubious means.
- Revenge against an enemy.
- Exiled forever.
- Adopted and brought up by pirates after some tragedy happened to their parents.

An enjoyable variation of this last one is finding out that you are the son or daughter of a famous pirate and that you inherit their ship and crew when you come of age, which brings us to –

Minor characters – Assembling the crew

Every pirate captain needs a crew. In a short story, introducing too many characters makes them difficult to keep track of and slows down the action. Having two or three minor characters, each given a name and a few descriptive details and personality traits, is preferable.

Activity

- Ask the children to write a descriptive sentence for some or all of these characters.

- Brainstorm further characters by giving them one or two of the traits mentioned below. What situations in a pirate adventure would bring out these characteristics?

Cowardly	Fierce	Jealous	Foolish
Nervous	Lazy	Brave	Risk taker
Grumbling	Eager	Strong and silent	Funny
Loyal	Excitable	Mutinous	Curious
Stupid	Cynical	Greedy	Puzzled

- Ask the class to come up with further adjectives that they can add to the descriptions they've already written or use to create new characters.

- Use an online 'pirate name generator' (see 'References and resources') to match names with the illustrations above and/or characters that the children have created.
- Match character traits with feelings. Traits tell us more about who a character is, defining aspects of their personality. Feelings are a character's emotional response to any given situation.

Traits	Feelings
1. Careful	a) Regretful
2. Sensitive	b) Shocked
3. Patient	c) Annoyed
4. Confident	d) World weary
5. Protective	e) Jealous
6. Optimistic	f) Embarrassed
7. Mean	g) Surprised
8. Stuck up	h) Desperate
9. Determined	i) Angry
10. Athletic	j) Scared
11. Inconsiderate	k) Confused
12. Kind	l) Worried
13. Independent	m) Relieved
14. Nosy	n) Anxious
15. Generous	o) Uneasy
16. Bossy	p) Happy
17. Brave	q) Nervous
18. Shy	r) Proud
19. Thoughtful	s) Thrilled
20. Rude	t) Sad
21. Authoritative	u) Discouraged
22. Proud	v) Hopeful
23. Clever	w) Disappointed
24. Ambitious	x) Uneasy

Take it further

- Create 'Top Trump' characters. Pick a number of traits (not necessarily just from the list) and roll two dice to find a score between 2 and 12. Random selection will throw up some interesting character profiles, including contradictions, which children are then invited to explain.
- Play the 'would you rather' game. Would you rather be sensitive or independent, for example, and why? Use the list of traits and feelings to generate further ideas. Children can consider these options with regard to themselves or characters they are creating.

● Ask children to create a character wheel. This is a circle divided into a number of segments: children can choose how many based on the complexity of the character they want to think about. Each segment represents a character trait, while the thickness of the 'slice' indicates how prominent that trait is in the character's behaviour. Children then fill the segment with feelings associated with that trait and situations where the trait and feelings are expressed. A mixture of written and drawn ideas makes for a colourful display.

You can invite children to complete the example character wheel or start from scratch. This is also an opportunity to introduce or revisit abstract nouns and adjectives.

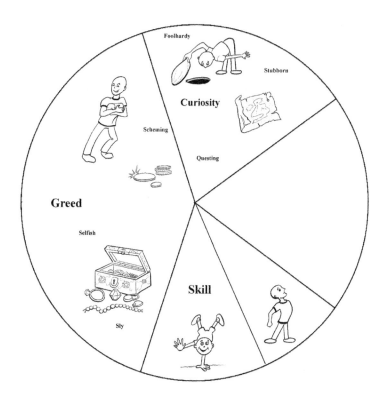

● Choose another genre to practise one or more of the activities above.

Then and now

This is simply a comparison between the modern-day and the times within which a conventional pirate story would be set. Begin with a brainstorming session where the children contribute ideas about how the two times differ. As ideas thin out, focus their thinking further by suggesting a number of topics: transport, the home, clothing, medicine, crime and punishment etc.

Record the children's ideas and use them as the basis for generating subsequent questions. Under the heading of 'medicine', for example, one Year 6 class came up with the following –

- Did any illnesses exist then that don't exist now, and vice versa?
- Were there hospitals in pirate times?
- What medicines existed then?
- Were there sinks, baths, showers and toilets in pirate times?
- Did doctors exist then and if so did they go to medical schools to train?
- Were disabled people treated equally and with respect, as we try to do now?

Research will uncover the answers to many of the children's questions, while some of the information they discover can be displayed as a class timeline.

Vocabulary, anachronisms and the plasticity of language

Some fictional genres are ideal for introducing new vocabulary and discussing other language-related ideas. With regard to pirate adventures, explain these and other terms to the class and encourage the children to use them in their stories –

- Boatswain (bos'n). This person would be in charge of several junior officers and share with them the responsibility for overseeing crew members' duties and morale, and for ensuring that the ship was well maintained. The word itself derives from the Old English *batswegen*, from 'bat' (boat), and the Old Norse *sveinn*, meaning 'boy'. The contraction to bos'n (or bosun) can be used as an example of how many words in our language are shortened – perhaps to make communication quicker, or maybe out of laziness?
- Cooper. A cooper is a barrel maker, whose work aboard ship would ensure that gunpowder was kept dry, food was kept sealed off from rats and liquids such as fresh water and alcohol were stored in leak-proof containers. Cooper is one of many examples of a surname deriving from a trade. Can children think of or find out about others?

- Cutlass. This is a short sword with a flat, slightly curved blade used more in a skirmish for cutting and slashing rather than thrusting or stabbing. The word derives from the Latin *cultellus*, meaning 'a small knife', and shares its root with 'cutler' and 'cutlery'.
- Flintlock. This is a term referring to any gun fired by striking a spark from a flint.
- Quartermaster. An elected position, the quartermaster was the captain's second-in-command, a foreman who was in charge of maintaining order, sharing out rations and supplies and handing out work duties.
- Powder monkey. This term referred to youths who made up most of the gun crews aboard ship. They were often forced into service and were usually very badly treated. Many would have tried to jump ship and desert if they had not been killed in battle beforehand.

A pirate ship would also number among its crew carpenters, cooks, gunners, musicians and possibly surgeons.

Take it further

- When looking at science fiction stories, ask the children to think what features of our own times would be anachronistic in the future. Point out how technology even today is developing rapidly, and that the pace of change is likely to accelerate. So for instance, within our lifetime radios with valves have been superseded by those using transistors, which have now evolved into DAB radios (digital audio broadcasting).
- Language evolves through time. It is not fixed or static. Words come into and drop out of use and their meanings can change. Ask children what the following words mean and then reveal their original meanings –
  - Awful meant something that was worthy of awe.
  - Clue (clew) used to mean a ball of yarn.
  - Girl once meant a child of either sex.
  - Guy is an eponym (named after a person) based on Guy Fawkes.
  - Meat used to refer to solid food of all kinds.
  - Naughty comes from 'naught', which means nothing or having nothing.
  - Nice originally meant silly, foolish or simple.
  - Pretty once meant crafty or cunning, later shifting to refer to someone who was clever or able.

- Look at terms related to computers and smartphones. Ask children to find out what they mean (unless they already know) and where the words come from. For example – byte, cookie, email, Internet, Google, malware, virus, wiki, zip.

See also page 126.

Romanticising

This occurs when we look at the past 'through rose-tinted glasses', making things seem better than they really were. Romanticising can apply to a period of historical time or it might be a personal trait relating to one's own past, the 'good old days syndrome'. In the context of helping children to write stories based on pirates, you might feel it's worth mentioning that many tales depict them in a romanticised way and that the pirate life was often actually more brutal and violent. Thus, romanticising is a kind of distortion of reality. Once children realise this you can use the notion to introduce subtler concepts, such as bias and the way emotive/persuasive language attempts to influence our view.

Treasure map

The treasure map is a common feature of pirate adventures and can provide a rich source of ideas for creative writing –

- Trying to find the island lends itself to the 'quest narrative' incorporating the basic story elements that we looked at on page 35.
- The pirates' difficulties can be increased by storms, high seas, thunder and lightning, winds that blow the ship off course, other bands of pirates also looking for the treasure etc. Further challenges and dangers can be encountered when our brave crew have reached the island.
- Treasure hunting tales create the opportunity to introduce children to the names of different geographical features, perhaps with some background information about them.
- In such stories the treasure can only be found by solving puzzles and riddles – see below.

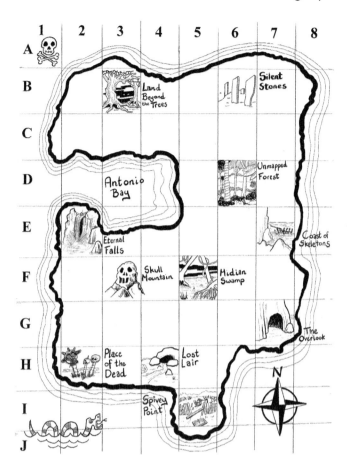

- We've buried three treasure chests on Puzzle Island. Can the children crack these clues to discover their location?

1. My first (letter) is in shiver and also in shake.
    My second's not in biscuit but always in cake.
    My third's to be found in you not in I.
    Fourth, fifth – to see these hunt low, low not high.
    You'll need wits, my friend, if it's treasure you seek.
    Use your head and your eyes, go on, take a peek.

Solution –

You can help children by explaining that each of first four lines gives a clue about a letter that features in the name of the place where the treasure is to be found.

The first line hints that the first letter of the place name is also the first letter of both 'shiver' and 'shake'.

The fourth line gives the clue to both the fourth and fifth letters of the place name, which are hinted at by the repetition of the word 'low'.

The sixth line mentions 'head' and 'peek', which is a homophonic pun on 'peak'.

So, the treasure is buried on Skull Mountain.

2. Before you start.
   Go east – then don't ignore insolent Tess.
   Wait until the sun's at its highest, then walk that way $12 - 2 + 8 \div 3$.
   Then, where the sun sets walk two – all riots will show you the treasure.

Solution –

'Before' is a pun on B4, where you start.

'Insolent Tess' is an anagram of 'Silent Stones'

The sun's at its highest in the south. Go six squares that way (the answer to the Maths puzzle).

The sun sets in the west. Go two squares. 'All riots' is an anagram of 'Lost Lair'.

You can award points for each part of the solution groups manage to solve.

3.

S	S	A	L	T	U	C	Q	G	K	Y	O
X	T	U	D	V	B	C	R	E	W	I	Q
P	J	N	H	L	A	D	D	A	R	T	S
A	Z	G	I	K	R	I	X	O	H	K	M
R	E	V	J	O	U	A	O	N	U	F	V
R	R	Q	U	A	P	K	F	L	R	Z	O
O	U	V	Q	T	P	Y	L	B	E	R	Y
T	S	G	C	J	I	U	E	I	I	H	A
N	A	P	T	N	R	D	Y	V	P	W	G
Q	E	O	X	S	A	Y	W	U	I	O	E
K	R	E	A	G	T	S	E	U	Q	P	B
T	T	L	N	O	E	L	L	A	G	M	S

S	S	A	L	T	U	C	Q	G	K	Y	O
X	T	U	D	V	B	C	R	E	W	I	Q
P	J	N	H	L	A	D	D	A	R	T	S
A	Z	G	I	K	R	I	X	O	H	K	M
R	E	V	J	O	U	A	O	N	U	F	V
R	R	Q	U	A	P	K	F	L	R	Z	O
O	U	V	Q	T	P	Y	L	B	E	R	Y
T	S	G	C	J	I	U	E	I	I	H	A
N	A	P	T	N	R	D	Y	V	P	W	G
Q	E	O	X	S	A	Y	W	U	I	O	E
K	R	E	A	G	T	S	E	U	Q	P	B
T	T	L	N	O	E	L	L	A	G	M	S

Note that hidden words might be written backwards, vertically up-down, as well as down-up or diagonally. 'Pirate-related' words that have nothing to do with the location of the treasure also appear in the puzzle.

Before starting, you can award each group a certain number of points and set a time limit of the same number of minutes. Groups lose one point after each minute has passed. Or simply award points for words found.

The third cache of treasure is buried at Spivey Point. Other hidden words are: crew, cutlass, galleon, parrot, quest, treasure, voyage.

Word searches help children to develop their concentration and think carefully about spelling, especially if you ask them to create word search puzzles of their own.

Take it further

- Children can bury treasure of their own and devise riddles and puzzles as clues to its location. They can add other place names to make the task more challenging. Groups swap puzzles and try to find their classmates' treasure.
- Prompt children to ask questions about the map and/or use these –
  What might be found in the Land Beyond the Trees?
  In what sense might the Silent Stones be silent?
  How could Skull Mountain have come into existence?
  What does the word 'lair' mean? What could be lurking in there?
  Why might the Coast of Skeletons be so named?
  Why might The Place of the Dead be located at the southeast edge of the island?
- Suggest that children write a dramatic scene or complete a short story about the pirates' quest to find the treasure. Bear in mind that pirates were very superstitious and that they told legends of phantom ships, cursed treasure, sea serpents and vicious mermaid-like creatures luring ships to the rocks or sailors to their deaths. Or setting the scene on an uncharted island could be another starting point. Almost anything could be there. Ancient overgrown temples where there is a fabulous jewel bearing a fearsome curse, strange and fearsome creatures, a marooned sailor with a harrowing tale to tell, an island of zombie slaves with a sinister master, innocents in need of rescue. Who knows?

Tip There are plenty of other historical periods which have captured the public imagination well enough to have developed a familiar iconography and some well-known tropes: Vikings, the American West, Roman times, knights, the streets of Victorian London. All places and times that capture the imagination and lend themselves well to narrative writing.

Note

1 The term 'swashbuckling' comes from the sixteenth-century term 'swash', which is to strike something violently, while a buckler was a small round shield that could be strapped to the forearm. A swashbuckler is, therefore, someone who makes a loud noise to intimidate by hitting his own or an opponent's shield.

6 Writing a thriller story

Summary of the chapter

- Definition of a thriller and its subdivisions. Distinction between thriller, chiller and mystery.
- Tips for what to include in a thriller.
- 'Two cool C's' to put in a thriller – confrontation and careering.
- Activity: Surprise Yourself. A brainstorming game to start with a bang or freshen up a flagging plot.
- Activity: Word Box. A writing challenge using random words.
- Activity: Finding a Focus. Reflecting on plot, characters, themes, suspense.
- More on dilemmas. Developing the skill of building dilemmas into a thriller story.
- Activities: Character webs and character grids. Showing children how to deepen their characters and explore relationships between characters in a story.
- Character motivations.
- Show, don't tell. Exploring this vital distinction when writing fiction.
- Activity: The 12-panel game. A visual tool for helping children to write short, taut, suspenseful scenes.
- More on pace, including looking at hooks and cliffhangers.
- Activity: Subplots. Introducing the idea and using the 12-panel game to generate some subplot ideas.
- Activity: Shout lines – Phrases or sentences to tempt the reader into the story.
- Kickstarters. Some first lines for thriller stories.

Definition of a thriller

A thriller is a story featuring a crime, a mystery or one that is set in the world of spies and espionage. These elements can occur together. As such, it is an overarching genre since by this definition it could be written as a science fiction tale, a fantasy, a historical story etc. The 'golden thread' that runs through thrillers is that they aim to create feelings of suspense, excitement, surprise, anticipation and apprehension.

Some writers make a distinction between thriller and mystery, suggesting that a mystery features a protagonist who puts clues together to solve a crime after it's been committed, while a thriller focuses on preventing some kind of wrongdoing from happening. You may or may not wish to point this out to the children: what's really important is that their stories should deliver thrills.

So, what's in a thriller?

Features of a good thriller are –

- Action. Keep the action moving. In planning and in writing, constantly ask, 'What happens next?' Having said this, *unrelenting* action throughout can become tedious, so young writers need to control and vary the pace of events. Also, thrillers often start with a bang – the reader is dropped straight into the action. More on this later.
- Maintain high stakes. In other words, characters are often at risk; the hero operates in a dangerous environment and is constantly thinking what is to be gained or lost by any possible course of action.
- Unpredictability. Deliver some shocks. Many if not all readers think ahead when reading a story, predicting what they believe will happen. Events suddenly turning out differently can therefore come as a pleasant surprise. However, one way of creating suspense in a story is to let the reader know what is about to occur while the hero and/or other characters remain ignorant. When the bad guys have destroyed a bridge up ahead and the hero is madly chasing after them on a stormy night, unaware that he or she might be about to plunge into a chasm, readers will be on tenterhooks if they know this; relieved when the hero spots the danger in time; and horrified if the hero's vehicle does indeed zoom headlong over the cliff. Again, it's about the

writer carefully controlling the unpredictable versus predictable features of a story – which, like just about every other writing skill, comes with practice and experience. This idea of allowing readers to know what the protagonist doesn't know is also called giving the reader a lofty viewpoint. It is one reason for writing in the third person in a thriller story.

- Dilemmas. A dilemma is a situation where a character must decide between two (sometimes more) unpleasant alternatives. So now our bad guys imprison two characters who are friends of the hero in different parts of a large abandoned warehouse. The villains have set explosives to demolish the building in five minutes. The hero is aware of the situation. They *may* be able to rescue both friends, though this means that the villains escape. By leaving both friends to their fate, the bad guys can definitely be caught. What should the hero do? Can the children come up with an inventive solution where both friends are rescued and the villains are caught?

- Have a time limit. The situation above is a perfect example of combining a dilemma with the fact that the protagonist must make a decision and act quickly. This creates tension for the reader, which is further heightened if the hero *doesn't yet know* about the forthcoming danger but learns of it when there is even less time to spare.

- Complications. Making situations even more complicated and difficult for a character supports all the other aspects of the thriller we've looked at so far... As the hero hurries to rescue the two friends (he can pick up the villains' trail later), he trips over some rubble, badly spraining his ankle. Can he now rescue both prisoners, or in trying will they and he perish? Or what if, on coming upon the explosives, the hero sees that the villains have left a message telling him that there are in fact two lots of explosives in the warehouse?

- Build to an exciting climax. One of the prisoners manages to free herself. She locates the (limping) hero, and together they find the other friend and all three of them manage to leave the warehouse and dive for cover just before the building explodes. In thrillers especially, the 'grand finale' should happen as close to the end of the story as possible. In other words, don't follow up with lengthy explanations or tying up other loose ends. A brief rounding off to the story will do... The hero and friends, exhausted and filthy, stagger into a nearby burger bar and order supper, much to the astonishment of the other diners. This creates a little light relief after the high drama of the story's climax.

- Transformations. In the chapter on writing fantasy, we looked at the idea of the journey as one of the basic narrative elements of a story (page 35). This often means a physical journey to dangerous locations, but it also means a transformative experience for the hero and perhaps for other characters too. One aspect that you might want to explore with the children is how the hero has changed by the end of the tale. Does he value his friends, who almost died, even more now? Is she even more determined to fight the forces of evil? Does their friendship grow even closer after the ordeal? A short piece of dialogue or a one-sentence description ('after all their disagreements, he nervously put out his hand to hold hers') can suffice and can fit nicely even into a short story.

Confrontation and careering

One of the most basic themes in fiction is the battle between good and evil. It lies at the base of the story pyramid (page 74) and lays the foundation for endless tales across the whole range of genres. (Incidentally, the word 'tale' is linked with the Dutch *taal*, meaning 'speech', and the German *zahl*, meaning 'number'. We pick up the sense of this in the modern term 'bank teller'.)

Confrontation usually takes place between the chief protagonist and the chief antagonist, hero versus villain, though all kinds of other confrontations can happen as a result of the main clash. In a thriller no less than in other genres, confrontation takes place in a high-stakes environment. Both hero and villain have a huge amount to lose if the other wins the day.

The tension and drama created by such a confrontation are heightened, and the story itself becomes more believable if the hero is not completely good and the villain isn't totally bad (or mad). An utterly good hero makes for rather a bland character. The defeat of a 100% evil villain fails to move us, apart perhaps from a fleeting sense of 'well thank goodness he's out of the way'. Encourage children when planning characters (see page 143 in this chapter and look at the checklist for other ideas) to give the hero some character flaw and/or a shadowy side to their personality. Also, get young writers to think about some trait in the villain that we can identify with so that they become a little more human.

The ancient yin-yang symbol illustrates the idea well. Here we have darkness and light in eternal relationship or entanglement. This represents the never-ending struggle between good and evil in narrative. One couldn't exist without the other. And yet, within the light there is darkness, and vice versa.

In explaining these ideas to children, point out that the darkness-in-the-light could be more of a vulnerability within the hero rather than some evil streak in their character. So maybe the hero lost a childhood friend that the villain resembles in some way. This would cause the hero to hesitate perhaps and so give the villain an advantage.

It's also worth bearing in mind that the full value of putting time and effort into planning a character may not be realised within a single short story. Characters that have depth can be used across a range of stories – the hero in a thriller, for example, can be renamed, given a fresh set of clothes and crop up in a fantasy tale. When writers do this, the characters take on greater realism and complexity. In subsequent stories, these come to the fore often in small ways: the writer's greater knowledge of such a character influences how the author causes the character to react, without taking up space in lengthy explanations. We call the notion of a character evolving through a number of stories a 'character type', which is the opposite of a stereotype, where characters are used 'off the peg' with little thought as to their depth and individuality.

Activity

● When the children have built up a character profile using any of the ideas in this book, ask them to bear in mind how that person (or creature!) can change over the course of a story and to make a note of that in their writing journals or on the character planning template itself.

Careering. The usual sense of the word is 'to move quickly in an uncontrolled manner' in the way a car with brake failure would go careering down a steep hill. However, because writing is a controlled process we're thinking more of a roller coaster ride, where the entire structure is set up to deliver a controlled but exhilarating ups-and-downs experience. To the reader a thriller story will feel like a roller coaster ride, whereas the writer will have constructed it to be stimulating but safe. Interestingly, the basic narrative template on page 38 fits the metaphor of the roller coaster beautifully.

The exciting ups-and-downs feel of a good thriller, as we said earlier, comes about through fast, but not unrelenting, action and some surprises coupled with a lofty viewpoint where appropriate, so that the reader knows what's coming but the characters don't. Ian Fleming, creator of the spy thriller stories featuring James Bond, said that his main aim was to get the reader to keep turning the page. And that really is the bottom line when trying to write thrillers.

Activity

● 'Maybe' thinking. As a warm-up to the 'Surprise Yourself' activity, show the class the picture of the speeding car and say, 'The men in the sports car are zooming away, maybe because…?' And invite the children to come up with as many alternative scenarios as possible. You can extend the activity by switching genres as ideas start of thin out. So, collect scenarios as though the scene was from a thriller story, then switch perhaps to science fiction, then fantasy etc.

Activity – Surprise yourself

● Show the children this list of situations. Consider them one at a time and think of three things that could happen next. Ask each child to write down their three ideas on a piece of paper and swap with a classmate who must try and think of one or two other ideas. Children then swap the papers back. Gather all the different situations the children have thought of and put them up on the board. This demonstrates that in writing there are always plenty of options. It also helps the children to think in multiples, rather than 'this happens next', 'this-or-this-or-this-or-this could happen next'.

1. A car comes speeding out of a side road and zooms towards you.
2. You are walking through an empty office block late one evening when suddenly all the lights go out.
3. Someone you've never met before suddenly runs at you and pushes you hard. You stumble away.
4. You are a guest at an awards ceremony honouring a number of important people. As one guest takes the stage, someone at the back of the hall screams out.
5. Walking home one evening you hear rustling in some bushes nearby. Curious, you go over to take a look and see…?

Activity

● Be unpredictable. We suggested earlier that thrillers (short stories especially) should jump straight into the action. Here are some opening scenarios – how many more can the children add to the list?

1. A lorry smashes through the wall.
2. A helicopter flies by, dropping thousands of leaflets on the town.
3. A strange green cloud billows along the street.
4. For no apparent reason, all the shop windows along the High Street shatter.
5. Everyone walking in the park suddenly starts dancing, but there's no music.
6. Dozens of cats gather in your neighbour's garden.
7. At night, floating lights in the sky arrange themselves into a slowly turning circle.
8. You hear bumping and scraping sounds coming from the empty house next door.
9. A group of masked men hurl bags of money *into* the local bank.
10. Unexpectedly, an announcer on your new TV set begins talking to you personally.

Take it further: Split the class into small groups. Ask each group to pick a scenario from the list, or one of their own, and develop it into a thriller story line. The story line planning technique on page 9 will work well for this.

Activity

● Word Box. This is an ongoing activity where children write words at random during spare moments in class (if there are any!) and drop them into the box. Different parts of speech can be written on differently coloured scraps of paper. If children need an idea for a story, or to move a story on, they come and pick one or two of the words. Tell children not to change their minds – once the words have been taken out of the box, they must be used. Some children might tell you that they couldn't think of any ideas. Suggest that they build an association web around one of the words or form a word chain linking two of the words they've selected. For example, picture and hat –

Picture – paint – tin – lid – on top – hat.

It doesn't matter if, like ours, a child's word chain is a bit forced. What matters is that she is making connections, this being one of the key aspects of creative thinking. If a child can't create a word chain, ask her to use two linked words in a sentence, which is much easier – 'I saw a picture of a hat'.

The word box activity uses randomness to spark ideas. The writer and polymath Edward de Bono has said that introducing the random factor stimulates creative thinking and dampens the tendency to 'try hard' to have ideas. The principle is similar to that of trying to remember a name that's on the tip of your tongue. The harder you try, the more the name seems to slip out of reach. But when you stop struggling, very often and usually quite quickly the name pops into mind. Creative thinking relies on ideas and experiences that lie at a subconscious level of the mind. Conscious effort inhibits the flow of information from the subconscious, whereas using randomness in thinking allows creative connections to be made subconsciously, which are then brought into conscious awareness. This is why when writing 'flows', it seems effortless and certainly feels more satisfying than consciously struggling to put sentences together.

Take it further

- Have a number of boxes available: one for first lines, one for story titles, one for brief story outlines etc. The children can drop ideas into these whenever they like, contributing to a growing resource whenever they need a little boost to their thinking.
- Story cubes. These are sets of picture dice that you roll out on the table and then try to build the pictures into a story line. Sets of reasonably priced blank dice are also available, allowing children to use their own words and/ or pictures.
- Story grids. In our opinion, the advantage of a story grid is that all of the information is visually available throughout the activity. Thus, children will be assimilating the words and/or pictures right across the grid even before they begin rolling dice to choose items at random. In other words, they will be making creative connections subconsciously and so are more likely to have further ideas popping into mind as the dice rolling proceeds.

Activity

- Finding a focus. This is a planning technique that asks children to think ahead around specific aspects of their story: plot, characters, theme and suspense. The focusing technique helps children to build their ideas into a more robustly constructed narrative and gives them a definite series of intentions to guide their writing. Ask children to consider the following –
  - Plot focus. The purpose of this scene is to...? (Set the time and place, introduce a character, develop characters through dialogue, heighten tension etc.)
  - Character focus. When readers finish this scene, they should feel...? (Relieved that the hero's friend is out of danger, unnerved because of the hero's situation, pleased that justice has been done etc.)
  - Theme focus. When readers finish this scene, I intend that they should think...? (That justice and the law are not always the same, that some people never change, that friendship brings out the best in people etc.)
  - Suspense focus. When readers finish this scene, I intend that they should wonder...? (If the hero and the person they saved will stay friends, that courage is about being frightened but going ahead anyway, if danger brings out the best in people etc.)

More on dilemmas

Building at least one moral dilemma into a story brings these benefits –

- Causes anguish in the characters and involves the readers more as they consider what they would do in that situation.
- Combined with the 'high-stakes' aspect of a thriller, the dilemma ramps up the tension and excitement.

Ask the class to brainstorm some dilemmas that could be used in a thriller story or use an extract from a story that reveals a dilemma but not its resolution. Show them these possibilities –

1. Best possible outcome.
2. Worst possible outcome.
3. Outcome that looks good but is in fact bad.
4. Outcome that looks bad but is in fact good.
5. Outcome that goes against something the character believes in.
6. Outcome that enables a character weakness to flourish.

You can either discuss various options in each category with the class or invite every child to roll a die and think about that outcome or outcomes before sharing ideas with each other. As with some of the activities using randomness that we looked at earlier, using dice rolls here can spark some fresh ideas.

A best possible outcome might be revealed at the end of a story to leave the reader with a feeling of satisfaction – Aha! So the villain got their comeuppance after all. However, if the outcome happens earlier in the story it can be used to give the hero a false sense of security or overconfidence that backfires later, pride coming before a fall.

A worst possible outcome, say a defeat for the hero, could make the hero more determined to succeed next time. Or, if the outcome occurs earlier, it might prepare the hero for a greater challenge later.

A seemingly good outcome that is actually bad puts the hero at a disadvantage. Perhaps they think they've won but then are taken by surprise and suffer a defeat, or come close to death before overcoming the villain.

A seemingly bad outcome that is actually good delivers an emotional impact to the reader. The author can play on this frustration or outrage, allowing the villain to gloat before the hero comes back stronger to win the day.

An outcome that goes against something the character believes in can create both inner and outer conflict (see page 147), allowing us to empathise with the character's soul-searching as we wonder what decision that person will make. There is an opportunity here to discuss with the children what they would do in that situation.

An outcome that highlights a character flaw and how that person deals with it is an effective way of deepening the character for the reader. It also creates an opportunity to show that even the most heroic people are not entirely good (see the yin-yang metaphor on page 137).

Character webs and character grids

A character web is a visual planner that helps children to organise and focus their thoughts. The visual shows a rather simple and schematic design: children can label the different areas to suit their own purposes, while the central circle could be the 'world inside' image explained elsewhere (page 147). An online search will throw up plenty of other design ideas for character webs.

The activity can be taken further by discussing how the various aspects of the character's life are interrelated. How are their weaknesses related to their goals? How are their fears connected to their successes in life, and so on.

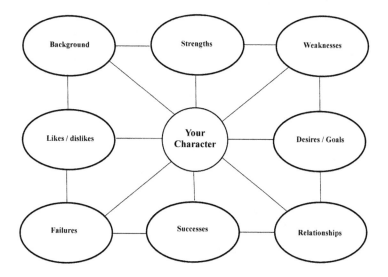

A character grid is designed to show the relationships between the dramatis personae of a story. Again, the device is very flexible and could accommodate a relatively large number of characters to include in a longer tale.

A quick and simple way of using the grid is to do some thinking about the characters first. Then think of a situation where the characters would meet. Imagine them jumping into the appropriate box – What would they say? How would they react to one another? What could they do in that situation (think of several ideas)?

As a warm-up to children constructing grids for their own stories, ask them to pick two characters from the grid below, imagine them coming together in the appropriate cell and having a conversation. What questions would they ask one another? What would they like and dislike about their sudden and fleeting companion?

	Winnie the Pooh	Harry Potter	Cinderella	Darth Vader
Winnie the Pooh				
Harry Potter				
Cinderella				
Darth Vader				

A more sophisticated version of the grid fills every box with comments about the other characters represented. A grid like this could be filled in during both the planning and the writing stage and complements the thinking children do with regard to developing character types (page 166).

	Alexis	Dean	Dimpul	Lian
Alexis	X	Feels that Alexis looks down on him and that she thinks she's perfect.	Admires Alexis, thinks she's strong and brave. Can be a bit envious of her.	Lian enjoys joking with Alexis, to take thoughts away from dangerous assignments.
Dean	She dislikes Dean greatly because he once failed to back her up when they were on a mission together.	X	Dean troubles her. He seems so resentful and rarely joins in socially.	Dean is a dark horse to Lian. She wonders what secrets he keeps hidden.
Dimpul	Gets on with Dimpul and feels protective towards her. Dimpul is clever but vulnerable.	Thinks that the girl is a bit of a wimp, but pleasant enough.	X	Dimpul is sweet and very bright. The team wouldn't work without her.
Lian	Very different but they work well together and get on socially.	Feels that Lian is distant and rather unfriendly.	Doesn't know Lian well, but thinks they could be good friends.	X

Character motivation

As we've seen elsewhere (page 40), for a story to be self-consistent, everything that happens must occur for a good reason, to strengthen the internal logic of the narrative. One aspect of this relates to the characters' motivations; they need believable reasons to drive what they do (this is why the evil genius wanting to take over the world because he's mad is such a weak idea).

Activity

- Look at Character Grid 2 above. Potential conflict exists between some of the characters, Alexis and Dean for example. Ask the children to pick two characters where potential conflict might occur; put those characters in a tense situation and think about how they would react. What would their motivation be for behaving as they do?

So for instance, if Alexis and Dean were sent on another dangerous mission and Dean gets into difficulty, would Alexis back him up if doing so would put her in danger too? On the one hand, she might if her loyalty to her agency was more important than walking away from peril. On the other hand, she might leave Dean to his fate out of revenge, or because before the crisis they obtained vital information that must be taken back to base.

Extend the activity –

- By looking at short stories or novels the children have read and picking out instances of the reasons behind what particular characters do in the situations they face.
- Thinking about motivations is an effective way of developing characters that have greater depth. Ask each child to pick a character they have invented (perhaps as a result of other activities in this book). Attach a blank sheet of paper to each character profile, then pass the profiles around the class. Children on receiving someone else's profile must now write down a 'what would your character do if...?' question that the creator of the character must think about when her profile is returned. (It would be unwieldy for all the children to look at all the profiles, so put a time limit of ten minutes or so on the exercise before profiles are returned.)
- Once children have thought about their list of 'what would your character do if...?' questions, ask them to decide what past experiences influenced their character so that they behaved in that way. In other words, begin to create a history for the character that supports logical and believable reasons for their present motivations. This could be done as a personal timeline, such as this one.

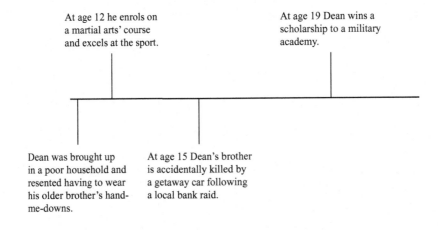

At age 12 he enrols on a martial arts' course and excels at the sport.

At age 19 Dean wins a scholarship to a military academy.

Dean was brought up in a poor household and resented having to wear his older brother's hand-me-downs.

At age 15 Dean's brother is accidentally killed by a getaway car following a local bank raid.

The inner world

While thrillers are all about action, and especially in short stories don't usually delve deeply into a character's personality, it's useful for children to have some idea about their characters' desires, concerns and feelings.

Show the class the visual and tell the children that the images within the circle are the things going on inside this boy's mind. Ask why he might be thinking of these things and why is he thinking of them in this way. Point out to the class if necessary that the images are representational rather than literal – the computer is not really that big with an angry face on the screen (see also metaphorical thinking on pages 120 and 177).

Take it further by asking children to make their own 'inner maps' for characters that they invent or those they've encountered in other stories. Supply circle blanks as templates: children can then draw, use clip art or images cut from comics and magazines to create a visual psychology for the character. Obviously, this technique can be used in any genre.

Show, don't tell

This is standard advice for writers. 'Show' means to try and create in the reader the same emotional experience that the characters have during the story. To say 'Dean was frightened' is simply to tell the reader about how he felt at that moment, whereas the writing would be more effective if we had some information about how Dean looked (body posture and facial expression), what his physiology was doing (pulse, breathing, muscle tension), how other characters were reacting and the dialogue between them.

To familiarise children with the 'show, don't tell' principle, ask them to fill in this template. They can work singly, in pairs or in small groups for this.

Show Don't Tell

1) Think of an exciting or scary situation.

2) Decide which characters are involved. You can use characters from stories you've already written or from other stories, or you can invent them now.

3) Pick one character to focus on.

4) Show how your character is reacting...

- What emotion is he / she feeling?

- What is your character's body posture and facial expression?

- How is your character reacting physically; heart rate, breathing etc?

- How is your character moving?

- What is your character saying?

- How is he or she saying this?

- What are the other characters saying?

Extend the activity by writing up the scenario in the 12-panel game below as though it were an extract from a story.

The 12-panel game

Originally appeared as Figure 13.1, Bowkett, S. *Using Comic Art to Improve Speaking, Reading and Writing*, 2016, re-produced with the permission of the publishers.

1. Show children the 12-panel scene. Point out that the panels are small, so the artist was only able to put in minimal details, tempting the reader's eyes to move quickly down the page. This creates a sense of drama, fast pace and tension. What else has the artist done to show these?
    - The 'action style' body language of the rescuer.
    - Returning repeatedly to the bomb-timer counting down and zooming in to highlight the imminent explosion.
    - Using 'action lines' in panel five as the rescuer smashes down the door.

    – Putting three 'ticks' in the penultimate panel to create an increased sense of time running out.

    – Ending with a cliffhanger in the final panel.

2.   Give out copies of the 12-panel blank sheet. Children can work individually or in pairs. Their task is to translate the visual action into words, fitting their text into the blank panels.

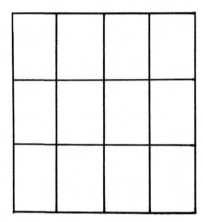

    Emphasise that children must choose their words carefully to maintain the fast pace and sense of drama. Remind the class to use forceful adjectives and strong verbs. Discuss whether the use of adverbs would enhance the pace or slow it down. Advise children to give the characters names before they begin.

    Other points to bear in mind –

● Choose which tense to write in. What are the advantages of using the past tense/present tense?

● Choose which person to write in (second person is also acceptable). Again, what are the advantages of writing in these different ways? (page 100)

● Visualise colours, sounds, smells and textures before writing. Decide how much detail needs to go in to enhance pace and tension.

● Consider how the characters are feeling. How much description of their emotions will the children put in?

3.   Once groups have finished, combine the most effective ideas to create a collaborative final version of the 12-panel text.

Take it further

- Create a vocabulary list of strong verbs, adjectives and adverbs. Show these when running the activity again with another group.
- What else could be put into the scene to make it more exciting? For instance, people pursuing the rescuer, boobytraps in the castle, overcoming guards.
- Experiment with different panel shapes for a variety of effects/reader responses. Ask the children to draw panels of different shapes and sizes. Discuss with the class how these might be used.
- If there was a 13th panel, what could it show to round off the scene or create an even more dramatic cliffhanger?
- Create short descriptions of each of the characters.
- Using the visual and textual versions of the scene, write it up in story form going into more detail but preserving the tension and pace.
- Enrich the plot with the 'cloud of questions' technique. Here, children are given a time limit of two or three minutes to ask as many questions as possible about the scene. Record the questions and subsequently create a 'short list' to answer (accepting more than one answer for each question if these are useful to build the plot).
- Cut-ups. Give out copies of the page of drawn panels, together with a page of blanks. Get children to cut out the panels and intersperse the drawn panels with blank ones that children write in to create –
  - A flashback.
  - The foreshadowing of future action.
  - A parallel plot featuring other characters in the greater story (see page 98 for more on these).
- If dialogue featured in the scene, what might the characters be saying to one another? How could different shapes of speech bubbles help to convey the characters' feelings?
- Again, if speech featured in the scene, how could punctuation be used to enhance the drama – the use of exclamation marks, dashes and ellipsis for example?
- Use the same scenario of a rescue, as depicted in the drawn scene, but change the genre to fantasy, science fiction, horror etc.

Hooks and cliffhangers

Most children will already understand the idea of cliffhangers – a dramatic and exciting finish to a scene that tempts us to read on. A hook serves the same function but happens at the start of a story, 'hooking' the reader's attention and interest immediately.

Activity

● Here are some ways of hooking the reader into a story. Ask the children to think of an opening sentence or paragraph for each kind of hook. These can apply to any genre, not just thrillers.

1. Begin at a critical moment.
2. Briefly describe an unusual situation.
3. Ask a fascinating question.
4. Introduce a startling or otherwise interesting character.
5. Begin with some interesting or dramatic dialogue.
6. Open with a puzzle or mystery.
7. Start with conflict – between two or more people, or inner conflict focusing on one character.
8. Introduce the villain.
9. Describe a sudden and dramatic change of emotion and what causes it.
10. Create a sense of wonder.

Here are some opening lines. Ask the children to decide which kind of hook they represent.

a) Without warning, and travelling at 60 miles an hour, the brakes of the car suddenly failed. (1)
b) The globe of blue light slowly turned a brilliant gold before zooming up into the sky. (6 or 10)
c) Alexis didn't know whether to risk her own life by trying to save Dean or simply walk away from the danger. (7)
d) Mr. Lee had a round head and the kindest smile I'd ever seen. He always wore brightly coloured waistcoats and multicoloured braces. (4)

e) So what could that shadowy shape in the woods really be? Alexis wondered. (3 or 6)

f) 'Hi, I'm here!' Lian called happily. She came up behind where her friend was sitting on the park bench and tapped her shoulder – only to feel a surge of horror as Dimpul slumped lifelessly to the ground. (9)

g) 'We meet at last, Dean'. Mr. Noir grinned triumphantly. 'But alas, all too briefly'. Then he raised his gun and fired. (1 or 8)

h) The team stood dumbfounded at the doorway of the cell. There was no way that Noir could have escaped, and yet now the room was empty. (6)

i) They reached the castle turret. It was a 50-foot drop to the moat below, but they couldn't hesitate – the bomb would explode at any second. (1)

j) 'It's ours for the taking', Hitchkett said. Bowman nodded, grinning. 'A million pounds' worth of uncut, untraceable diamonds'. (5)

Some of the hook categories work for cliffhangers too. One useful technique for developing the skill is to write or find a cliffhanger sentence and think about what happened immediately beforehand using the 3-2-1 technique.

3) Cliffhanger – They stood on the castle turret staring at the dark waters of the moat 50 feet below.

2) Before that – Dean dragged the semiconscious Alexis up off the floor and stumbled with her towards the stone staircase.

1) Before that – Dean smashed down the wooden door of the cell and hurried towards the girl slumped in the corner.

Now get the children to try the three-step method by using some of the sentences in the hook activity above. Point out that cliffhangers should be short and to the point, and that the writer should have thought about how the cliffhanger will be resolved; that is, how the next scene or chapter will start.

Take it further

How would these cliffhangers be resolved – in other words, what happens next?

● 'Hi, I'm here!' Lian called happily. She came up behind where her friend was sitting on the park bench and tapped her shoulder – only to feel a surge of horror as Dimpul slumped lifelessly to the ground.

- 'We meet at last, Dean'. Mr. Noir grinned triumphantly. 'But alas, all too briefly'. Then he raised his gun and fired.
- The team stood dumbfounded at the doorway of the cell. There was no way that Noir could have escaped, and yet now the room was empty.
- Without any warning the steering failed. Bowman's car veered off the road and went hurtling towards the sheer drop into the chasm.
- Footsteps echoed along the corridor. Then there came a crash and the door of the cell burst open. A silhouette loomed in the doorway.

Subplots

A subplot is a secondary strand that supports or adds to the main thread of a story. Subplots usually but not invariably involve more minor characters rather than the main protagonist or antagonist. The value of using subplots is that they can make fuller use of secondary characters such as the hero's or villain's partner (see 'Basic narrative elements' on page 35). Also, subplots generally require switching to a different scene. 'Toggling' between the main action and the subplot is an effective way of increasing pace and tension.

Activity

- Imagine that the scene featured in the 12-panel game on page 149 is part of the main plot of a thriller story, where the hero rescues a friend captured by the villain. Ask children to come up with some ideas for what might have led up to this point. Imagine too that earlier in the story we were introduced to the hero's partner, who was instructed to help the hero and friend to escape from the castle. How might the partner do this? For example, they might –
  - Be waiting below with a speedboat ready to whisk the others away.
  - Arrive in a helicopter and drop a rope ladder to the hero and friend as they reach the top of the castle turret.
  - Set up covering fire to help the others escape.
  - Create a diversion of some kind, using smoke bombs maybe.
  - Arrive with the police (or FBI etc.) to round up the bad guys in the nick of time.

Now ask the children how they would toggle between the main plot and the subplot to make this part of the story as exciting as possible. They can use the visual and write the subplot in the blank spaces we've chosen.

Alternatively, print off copies of the 12-panel scene and blanks, get children to cut them out and arrange them along a story line to show the sequence of events. Our example mirrors the visual above, but the children can arrange their subplot panels just as they wish.

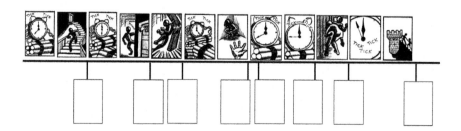

- Imagine that the drawn panels *form the subplot* of the story. Ask the children to come up with ideas for a main plot that would fit in with the rescue of the prisoner in the castle.
- If the children have written stories from other genres, ask them to look back at their work to see if a subplot would make the main story more interesting and exciting.

Shout lines

A shout line is an intriguing phrase or sentence that aims to tempt the reader into the story. You often find shout lines on the front cover of a book or DVD case. Typing 'shout lines for children's books' into a search engine will pull up plenty of examples, such as –

'Can you really love with a heart of stone?' (*Grey* by Christi J. Whitney).

'The stakes are high and each may have to pay with the highest price of all – their life' (*The Eagle of the Ninth Chronicles* by Rosemary Sutcliffe).

'A dragon prince in mortal danger' (*The Dragon Charmer* by Douglas Hill).

'What voices whisper to you on the Hallowmas wind? Step beyond the veil if you dare' (*Halloween Pie* by Ben Leech).

You'll see from these examples that a shout line may be in the form of a question that will be answered by reading the story. Or it can be ambiguous. In the third example, what kind of mortal danger does the dragon prince face? The fourth example is a direct challenge to the potential readers – are they brave enough to read the stories within?

Encourage the children to bear these points in mind as they tackle the activities below.

- Ask the children to devise shout lines for stories they've already written.
- What shout lines can they come up with for the thriller suggested by the 12-panel game (page 149)?
- Split the class into pairs. Their task is to look for examples of shout lines from children's books and films. Each pair then reveals their shout lines one at a time and the rest of the class suggest what those stories could be about.
- Ask children to pick a favourite story and create a suitable shout line. Or, where one already exists, suggest a suitable alternative.

Kickstarters

Here are some first lines for thriller stories. You might want children to plot the whole story, or just suggest a title or shout line, or create a blurb.

1. I'd only been away for two weeks, but when I got back everything had changed.
2. 'The security is likely to include heat sensitive triggers, keypad entry, handprint locks and multiple guards – good luck!'
3. And we watched as the beach lit up again and again with the flames of brightly burning fires.
4. Fog, thick and swirling, marked the entrance to the cave.
5. This is the most difficult mission we've ever tackled, Sam thought as the boat came round the headland and brought the castle into view.
6. He regained consciousness and found himself lying on the floor staring at the sinister figure looming over him.
7. I jump, tackle him and manage to disarm him before he can draw his gun.
8. 'Panicking is not the way to deal with this problem', Sasha said firmly.
9. Silently they crept through the woods towards the lights in the distance.
10. 'Why are you scared of her?' he wanted to know.

> **Tip** The counter flip game (page 34) will work well in helping children to create story lines from these kickstarter sentences.

7 Writing a Gothic horror story

Summary of the chapter

- Introduction. Definition of Gothic horror and its relationship to the broader genre of horror. Taking a brief look at Gothic style and tone in art, architecture and fashion. A short exploration of whether it's right for children to read and write horror stories.
- Features and conventions of Gothic horror.
- Tropes in Gothic horror stories – themes, people, places and objects that extend the section above.
- Introducing 'urban folktales' and using 'The Phantom Hitchhiker' as a way of approaching Gothic fiction. This section also defines 'flash fiction'.
- Character types in Gothic fiction. This section broadens out from considering just monsters to look at the rich array of character tropes in the subgenre.
- Stereotypes in Gothic fiction – for example, the helpless female in distress being rescued by the male hero – and how it's OK for young writers to challenge and change these. A brief look at parody.
- The evolution of the vampire as a trope.
- How to make a monster.
- Monsters as metaphors. A brief look at how vampires, werewolves and other creatures can represent aspects of the human psyche. Reflecting on this may lead to philosophical discussions on what it means to be human, how far we have free will (if at all) and what it means to live a moral existence. It also touches again on the perennial human theme of the conflict between good and evil.
- Romanticism and the pathetic fallacy – a relationship with nature.
- Further tips for writing Gothic fiction, including the 'photograph method' for structuring descriptive writing.
- Story starters. Some 'seed ideas' to get children thinking about stories of their own.

Introduction

Originally the adjective 'Gothic' referred to East Germanic peoples comprised of many ethnic groups, two of whose tribes, the Visigoths and the Ostrogoths, were instrumental in the fall of the Roman Empire during the 5th century AD. According to their own folklore they originated in Scandinavia before crossing the Baltic Sea in three ships to the southern shore, where they settled after defeating the Vandals and other peoples living in that area.

The term Gothic also refers to a style of architecture common in Western Europe during the 12th–16th centuries, a style that was revived in the 18th and early 20th centuries. Gothic architecture has been described as having a 'dark magnificence', typified by pointed arches, soaring vaults, flying buttresses, large windows and intricate traceries used decoratively.

During the last century and into this one, Gothic motifs have influenced art, music, film and fashion (see for example Roberts, Livingstone and Baxter-Wright, 2014, and Townshend, 2014). In literature, Gothic influences appear in the work of the great Romantic poets of the 18th and 19th centuries and the writing of novelists from Horace Walpole's 1764 novel *The Castle of Otranto* through Mary Shelley's *Frankenstein* (1819), Bram Stoker's *Dracula* (1897) and on into the present day, where the popularity of Gothic fiction has grown enormously.

In recent decades, 'goth' has become a lifestyle choice where (according to http://www.whatisgoth.com/) adherents 'find beauty in things others consider dark'. The website goes on to explain that goths are not evil, unkind, violent or lacking in humour; they just enjoy what is dark and mysterious. As such, they form a distinct cultural group, some of whose members have suffered bullying in and beyond school; this fact in itself creates the opportunity to discuss the issue of cultural diversity and conflict with your class.

In this chapter we want more clearly to define Gothic fiction and to point out how studying the subgenre and writing stories based on that study brings a number of benefits to the development of children's writing and more widely to their thinking. We understand that mere mention of the terms 'Gothic' or 'horror' might be controversial to some parents and teachers for various reasons. If this is how you feel then, as we explained in this book's main introduction, you can cherry-pick some of the activities and techniques you find in the chapter and use them within the context of another genre. (The same kind of controversy arose around the use of the *Harry Potter* books in some schools, with a number of parents wanting them banned. Typing the question 'Why is *Harry Potter* banned in some schools?' brings up a wealth of articles on the subject. The topic is ripe for children to debate, unless they're not allowed.)

The 'References and resources' section lists some websites that open up the discussion on whether children should be exposed to horror and by extension fantasy. Points in favour include –

- Such stories can be exciting to read and write – the argument of engagement.
- Horror and fantasy stories (like some fables) can be cautionary tales, highlighting the possible consequences of certain decisions and actions. A parent's wise advice not to talk to strangers, for example, makes an ideal theme for a horror story.
- Many horror stories, again like fables, are highly moralistic with good and evil being clearly delineated. Where this is not the case, children learn via the world of the story that good and evil, right and wrong, are sometimes not so clear-cut in the real world. Indeed, Gothic fiction reflects this greater complexity and ambiguity. The idea of the anti-hero is prominent in Gothic tales – with the proviso that such a character is not 'against' the hero as the prefix anti- implies, but rather might act heroically yet out of motives that are less than praiseworthy. Also, characters in these stories often transgress in some way. Gothic villains frequently break taboos or otherwise 'step over the line'. It hardly needs mentioning that many children do this also as they try and find out where various metaphorical 'lines' in their lives are drawn.
- A point closely connected with the above is that Gothic stories (and those in other genres) warn of the possibility of danger nearby, showing us that the world is not always safe. The message may be more or less implicit but amounts to 'stay alert, think before you act, know who your friends are and stick with them' – which is why a character's suggestion to 'split up and investigate' that we find in some horror stories is not such a good idea!
- A rather more abstruse function of horror stories is that they allow children to be 'safely scared' yet at some level to put a name to their fears and face them rather than suppressing them. Writing horror can serve as an even more powerful catharsis.
- On a lighter note, for children to write Gothic fiction – as with any genre – they need to learn about it. Reading books by authors such as R. L. Stine and Darren Shan can well lead to a wider interest, not just in horror but other genres of literature.

Reasons to be wary of exposing children to Gothic stories, and by extension horror, fantasy and fairy tales, include –

- Some stories of this kind attempt to scare readers into behaving in a particular way, rather than encouraging them to think about actions and consequences. In certain early versions of 'Little Red Riding Hood', for example, the wolf eats the child after she gets into bed with him and there is no hero to save the day. We might wonder therefore whether children should be exposed to such unwholesome scenarios. However, should 'sanitised' versions of the story where the woodsman appears, slays the wolf and saves the child be used to try and teach a lesson about life?
- Some fairy tales and horror stories portray stereotypes such as old, powerful scheming women who are evil witches and beautiful young maidens stumbling into difficulties and needing to be rescued by a man, often a handsome prince. (To address this point, later in the chapter we aim to make children more aware of stereotypes like these and to question them.)
- Some adults object to children reading 'scary' stories on religious grounds, feeling that it's wrong for children and young people to be exposed to the occult or paranormal in any form.

These viewpoints can be challenged to some extent by realising that children's exposure to material in any medium or genre needs to be age-appropriate, and that young readers/writers become more confident and resilient when they are taught to think, reflect, question and discuss. The very fact that we have included this chapter in our book confirms that we approve of children learning about Gothic fiction rather than adults forbidding it.

Finally, the philosopher Alain De Botton (De Botton, 2014, p. 193) distinguishes between what he calls horror and tragedy. De Botton defines horror as a meaningless narration of revolting events, whereas tragedy (which might be just as gory and violent) is an educative tale 'fashioned from abominations'. Thus, some of Shakespeare's plays, Greek plays and the finest of what we normally think of as horror/Gothic literature would fall into this category.

We raise the point to reinforce the notion that horror as we broadly think of it is really composed of a continuum of narratives, beginning from gratuitously nasty pulp fictions to tales with an almost mythic quality that aim to communicate deep truths about what it means to be human.

All that said, many children might simply be interested in writing about zombies, rampaging werewolves and beautiful vampires straight out of Hollywood!

Features and conventions of Gothic fiction

As mentioned earlier, Gothic fiction is usually characterised by an air of gloom, mystery and darkness. A strong thread of Romanticism also runs through much of the literature (see page 178). Other common features are the use of 'distant narratives', which is to say the telling of the story through fictional diaries, letters, journals and accounts coming from a 'friend-of-a-friend'[1]. *Frankenstein* and *Dracula* are two prominent examples of the distant narrative technique. (Incidentally, abridged versions of these and other Gothic novels suitable for reading with children are available, for instance in the Ladybird Classics series).

We will look at urban myths later in the chapter, using one of the best known – 'The Phantom Hitchhiker' – as a vehicle for familiarising children further with Gothic fiction. For many other examples of urban myths and analyses of their place in folklore and psychology, see Brunvand (1981, 1989, 1993) and Goss (1984).

Gothic stories rely heavily on what has been called the 'vocabulary of gloom' to create and sustain their atmosphere. So we find frequent references to thunder and lightning, wind (which may be howling, although you might want to encourage children to be more original), lashing rain, wild and remote places generally, graveyards and tombs, gates and doors creaking on rusty hinges, sighs, moans, mysterious footsteps, night journeys, echoes, dogs baying, eerie sounds such as maniacal laughter, unexplained sobbing, shadows and darkness, lights on in empty buildings, ruins, trackless forests, bleak moorlands, mountain peaks, clouds streaming across the moon, thundering waterfalls and surging rivers.

These and other features of the landscape help to define and describe the Gothic 'flavour' of a story. We look at landscape in more detail on page 180. The element of mystery is evoked by the use of enchantment and magic, portents, omens, visions and predictions, nightmares, madness, secrets, amulets and talismans, coded messages, old and esoteric books, maps and scrolls, spirits, hauntings, science used for diabolical purposes and certain kinds of 'monsters' (see page 174).

Activity

- Ask children to suggest synonyms for, or words that are associated with, the following to build up a vocabulary bank they can draw on when writing their Gothic tales –

- Apprehension.
- Gloomy.
- Sorrow.
- Dismal.
- Dread.
- Hopelessness.
- Mournful.
- Wretched.
- Concern.
- Fearful.

Tropes in Gothic fiction

We've touched on some of these in the previous section, but here are more to help children enrich their Gothic worlds –

Banditry	Betrayal	Carnivals	Corruption
Envy	Exile	Fallen nobility	Fate
Fire	Fog	Forbidden things	Ghosts
Gypsies	Imprisonment	Immortality	Inheritance
Look alikes	Lost love	Masks	Mishaps
Murders	Promises	Revenge	Rituals
Secret tunnels	Theft	Transformation	Wandering

Activity

- Get the children to create a 'mood board' to represent visually the themes, settings, characters and other tropes in Gothic fiction. Use 'Mediaeval style' fonts for labels and extracts of text.

Urban myths

Urban or contemporary myths are rooted in popular culture and the oral tradition of storytelling. They are often humorous, horrific, bizarre, disgusting and usually have the ring of truth about them, purporting to have been recounted to the teller by a friend, who in turn heard it from his friend, and so on down the line. As such they are also called FoaF or friend-of-a-friend stories.

One of the oldest and best known is the tale of the phantom (or vanishing) hitchhiker. There are various versions, but basically the story tells of a man who is driving home late at night along a lonely country road when his headlights pick out a young woman thumbing a lift. He stops and offers to take her to her destination. She gets into the back of the car and gives him an address. The man glances at her in his rearview mirror a few times and notices how pale she looks, with dark rings around her eyes.

She obviously doesn't want to make conversation, but in a gesture of friendliness he asks if she has come a long way. When she doesn't reply, he glances in the mirror again and is shocked to see that she is no longer there. He wonders if she has curled up on the seat to sleep and stops the car to check that she's OK. His initial shock gives way to a growing puzzlement and a deepening sense of unease as he discovers that the girl has vanished. There was no way she could have opened the door and jumped out, so what happened?

To satisfy his curiosity, he drives to the address the girl gave him and knocks on the door. An older woman answers, and as the man recounts his tale the woman's face crumples and her eyes fill up with tears. She shakes her head and puts up a hand to stop him.

'I don't have any explanation', she says. 'All I can tell you is that from your description the young woman sounds like my daughter. And she was killed a year ago today by a hit-and-run driver – at the very spot you say you picked her up'.

(Strangely, as we were preparing this chapter we heard the story again. Our friend Ben Leech told it to us, having heard it from his second cousin who said that the older woman was his aunt.)

Activities

- What motifs in the story are you also likely to find in a Gothic tale?
- Ask the children to write a longer version of the story, giving the characters names, describing them and the setting in more detail and endeavouring to heighten the dark, lonely quality of the setting and the driver's sense of unease.
- 'Flash fictions' are very brief stories, perhaps just a couple of hundred words, that still feature a plot and some character development to make them more believable. They often aim to create immediate conflict and tension to grip

the reader. Ask the children to adapt 'The Phantom Hitchhiker' or another urban myth as a piece of flash fiction. Offer the following tips –

- Pick a single theme and stick to it. In other words, what big idea underpins the plot, and what do you want your readers to take from the story? (In the hitchhiker story, the theme could be that of loss or the unexplained.)
- Decide on a key emotion to establish the tone of the tale. (In our example, a little thrill of unease.)
- Have a definite plot with a beginning, middle and an end – don't just write an extract. Give the characters a reason for being there.
- Pick a main character and have all the action revolve around them. Limit the number of characters to no more than three.
- Try to keep everything happening in one locality; don't leap about from scene to scene. Also, limit the number of scenes.
- Cut out all unnecessary words.
- Write in the third person from just one character's point of view (i.e. don't jump from character to character. This is called 'head hopping').
- Jump into the story where the conflict starts. This will be a crucial moment in the main character's life where drama and tension are high. Avoid prologue and backstory.
- Show, don't tell. Make the reader feel what the main character is going through.
- Choose a memorable title.

● Now ask the children to look again at our version of 'The Phantom Hitchhiker' to see how far we've succeeded in following these tips. Where we have failed, how would the children use the advice to improve our story?

> **Tip** Folktales, legends and myths are a rich source of plots, characters, settings and other tropes that children can use in their own writing.

Finally, in this section we look at what might be called 'micro writing'. These are very brief scenarios that aim to deliver an emotional punch in two or three sentences. Ask children if or how far they find these examples to be creepy. Can they come up with any examples of their own?

● I thought the tapping on the glass was someone outside the window, until I realised it was coming from within the mirror.
● I chuckled at the painting of the glum-looking clown, until it began to smile at me.

- I heard the old woman muttering to herself through my bedroom wall. She died two years ago.
- I woke from the nightmare I'd had of the vampire hunting me, flopped over onto my back and saw it looking down at me from the ceiling.
- The picture on my phone showed me asleep in my bed. I live alone.
- The more I peered through the darkness at my dressing gown hanging on the peg, the more I convinced myself it was moving. 'Pull yourself together', I thought. A moment later the dressing gown flew towards me screaming.
- My 6-year-old son asked me to check for monsters under the bed as I tucked him in. I looked there and saw my boy staring back at me. 'Daddy', he whispered, 'there's somebody on my bed'.
- The horrible face grinned at me through the front room window. My apartment is on the 13th floor.
- I swung myself round to sit on the edge of the bed and began to yawn. Then a cold hand wrapped itself around my ankle.

Character types in Gothic fiction

Gothic fiction is rich with colourful and interesting characters. Here is a selection –

Academic	Adventurer	Beautiful Gypsy	Beggar	Black Widow	Clown
Corrupt Lawyer	Cruel Relative	Damsel	Demon Hunter	Evil Nobleman	Gentle Giant
Innkeeper	Inventor	Long Lost Heir	Lord	Lover	Madman
Nanny	Necromancer	Noble Savage	Orphan	Outcast	Peasant
Poet / Artist	Schemer	Seer	Servant	Skeptic	Stepmother
Pirate	Stranger	Trickster	Vampire	Werewolf	Wise Fool

The list is 'artfully vague'. That is to say, in each case a character is suggested, but enough creative space is left for children to add their own details. The technique works well when evoking mood and tension: it's creepier to say, 'I noticed something out of the corner of my eye' than 'I noticed a vampire out of the corner of my eye'. In the classic ghost story 'The Haunting' (1963, age rated 12 in the UK), the Professor and Luke are lured out of the rambling old house when they see a dog running along the passageway and then outside. But as the Professor later says, 'or something we *thought* was a dog'. Here the viewer's imagination gets to work trying to picture what the thing might have been. Like many techniques in writing, however, artful vagueness should be used sparingly for maximum effect.

Activities

● Create an association web around a chosen character type. This can be a group activity where children brainstorm ideas. You may want the web to be done in one go, or over time where the children accumulate ideas as they come to mind.

Tip Encourage the use of a dictionary and thesaurus when children are unsure of any of the terms, and as a prompt for generating further ideas.

Halloween

moon behind clouds

nighttime

eerie

shadows

lonely road

ghost.

woods

following   forests

mysterious

Stranger

at the door

bringing news

good   bad

long lost relative.

evil brother / sister / twin

message

prophecy

threat

● Some of the character types come with an adjective – beautiful gypsy, evil nobleman, gentle giant etc. Ask children to suggest adjectives to describe some of the noun-only character types. Extend the activity by asking them to select one or two others from the grid below.

Agreeable	Awestruck	Boastful	Brutal	Charming	Courageous
Deceitful	Deluded	Desperate	Evil	Exotic	Frightened
Greedy	Honourable	Innocent	Helpless	Loathsome	Lonely
Long-lost	Love-struck	Mad	Murderous	Mysterious	Nervous
Obsessive	Outspoken	Reckless	Ruthless	Scheming	Sinister
Stalwart	Stubborn	Tormented	Vain	Virtuous	Wicked

Stereotypes

Most of the traits in the grid refer to a character's personality. Invite children to come up with adjectives related to a physical description. This activity might be an opportunity to discuss stereotyping – the damsel might be helpless, the stranger might be sinister, the pirate might be reckless etc. Ask the children how these and other stereotypical characters would behave in the situations below.

> **Tip** Using dice rolls (pages 39 and 50) to match characters with traits will generate some novel ideas.

1. Being chased through woodland at night.
2. Trapped in a deserted old house.
3. Waking up to the sound of a strange voice.
4. Confronted by a menacing shadowy figure.
5. Hearing a child crying on a deserted street.
6. Getting lost on moorland as a storm threatens.
7. Being told by a fortune teller of an approaching personal crisis.
8. Being deserted by companions in a supposedly haunted house.
9. Being bitten by a vampire.
10. Finding a manuscript that can confer great power, but at a price.

A stereotype is a fixed and simplified portrayal of, in this case, a person. As with the use of clichés, stereotypes can be used unthinkingly in a story. So in Gothic tales we might find the frightened damsel in distress, the mad scientist, the hunchbacked loyal servant (called Igor), the fearless hero (who gets the girl) and the ruthless villain (with the maniacal laugh). Because stereotypical characters are familiar to many readers, they amount to a kind of shorthand: an author can use them 'off the peg', knowing that readers will readily fill in many details by association. Children using stereotypes in their stories is acceptable as they learn the craft and become familiar with the motifs and conventions of different genres, but over time young writers should be encouraged to think more deeply about their characters and break the stereotypical mould.

Activities

● Write a character-type on a scrap of paper. Prepare a vertical list of adjectives, at least one of which matches the stereotype. Pick a situation (perhaps from the list on page 168). Move the character down the list one step at a time and discuss how they would react in each case.

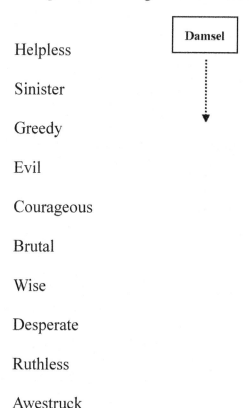

Being chased through a woodland at night...

Helpless

Sinister

Greedy

Evil

Courageous

Brutal

Wise

Desperate

Ruthless

Awestruck

● Split the class into groups to create an association web to add detail to character types. This kind of group brainstorming is also likely to generate plot ideas.

Parody and Gothic fiction

Parody is a form of satire where exaggeration and irony are used for comic effect to imitate the motifs and conventions of a genre or particular work. Any genre can be parodied, but we mention it in this chapter since many critics feel that Jane Austen's *Northanger Abbey* parodies the motifs and conventions of Gothic fiction.

The main learning benefits of looking at parody are that in order to achieve it, children will need a degree of understanding of how the genre works and of the effect that the style and tone of a piece of writing has on its readers. Deliberate exaggeration (or hyperbole) also makes children more aware of how it is used in everyday speech, where the unthinking use of superlatives can rob words of their emotional force.

● Begin by showing children some exaggerated sentences and ask how they could be toned down.
  – Tears poured down her face.
  – I hate brussels sprouts.
  – It's absolute chaos in this classroom today!
  – The film I've just watched was awesome.
  – That joke you told had me splitting my sides with laughter.
  – The drawing you've done is totally brilliant.
  – The wind screamed like a hurricane as it rampaged through the trees.
  – I've told you a million times to end a sentence with a full stop
  – It's OK for you – you've got tons of money.
  – Just because *you* think you've got a brain the size of a planet...

> **Tip** This activity also creates the opportunity to point out the difference between statements that are figuratively true and those that are literally true.

● Similarly, how might this overblown example be written in a more moderate way?

The horrifying figure shambled towards them through the torrential rain. Its claws looked like scimitars as they raked and slashed menacingly at the air. Lightning flickered with dazzling brilliance as though the heavens were splintering apart, then thunder boomed like an atom bomb, making the very earth tremble as though it too were terrified. Bowman shuddered with terror, his hair standing up on the back of his neck, his heart in his mouth, his blood freezing in his veins. Beside him Teresa let out an ear-piercing screech that almost burst her companion's eardrums. Her heart was pounding like a trip-hammer and her limbs quivered as though every muscle was twerking.

The evolution of the vampire trope

'The solemn tones of an old cathedral clock have announced midnight – the air is thick and heavy – a strange, deathlike stillness pervades all nature. Like the ominous calm, which precedes some more than usually terrific outbreak of the elements, they seem to have paused even in their ordinary fluctuations, to gather a terrific strength for the great effort. A faint peal of thunder now comes from far off. Like a signal gun for the battle of the winds to begin, it appeared to awaken them from their lethargy, and one awful, warring hurricane swept over a whole city, producing more devastation in the four or five minutes it lasted, than would a half century of ordinary phenomena'.

So opens *Varney the Vampire, or a Feast of Blood* probably written by James Malcolm Rymer (the attribution is questionable) between 1845 and 1847. It was serialised first as a penny dreadful (a cheap comic or book containing sensationalist stories) and then in book form, a volume amounting to a massive 232 chapters over 876 double-column pages: a free PDF copy is available at www. gutenberg.org.

The writing style is intentionally overblown, while the byline on the front cover announces that the tale is 'a romance of exciting interest'. Varney himself (itself?) is described as having a face that is 'perfectly white – perfectly bloodless. The eyes look like polished tin; the lips are drawn back, and the principal feature next to those dreadful eyes is the teeth – the fearful looking teeth'.

Rymer's novel paved the way for the hundreds of vampire stories that followed and envisioned the classic look that many associate with the undead. While Bram Stoker's later portrayal of Dracula is similar in some ways – 'a cruel-looking man with pointed teeth and ears, strong eyebrows, pale skin but lips of a startling redness' – the vampire as a motif has evolved and diversified over the years. In vampire tales of the 18th century, the creatures – nosferatu – derived from folklore and came from the peasant classes, living a rural existence, uneducated, dirty and having no appeal whatsoever for their victims. A work that predated *Varney*, John Polidori's *The Vampyre* (1819), portrayed the creature as a charismatic, isolated yet glamorous figure, a motif echoed in the Universal films of the 1930s starring Bela Lugosi and the Hammer movies of the 1970s with Christopher Lee as Dracula.

More recent incarnations (if we can use that term) include Anne Rice's genteel and beautiful vampires in *Interview with a Vampire: The Vampire Chronicles*, the angst-ridden teen punk vampires of Joel Schumacher's film *The Lost Boys* and the vicious and filthy creatures terrorising a snowbound Alaskan town in the movie *30 Days of Night* (2007). All are age rated over 12 years in the UK.

This brief overview is to offer you some background in preparation for the activities that follow, rather than sharing it with the children. However vampires remain popular with many young readers in children's literature, and an online search will bring up numerous titles appropriate to specific age ranges and reading ability. However, the same controversy over whether children should be exposed to horror stories relates also to vampire stories, with one commentator (who actually recommends various titles) announcing that the books will satisfy children's 'morbid young imaginations'. Since morbid means to take an unhealthy interest in something, we find the value judgement puzzling.

Activities

Here is the 'classic' and perhaps best-known portrayal of the vampire. Ask children to point out the stereotypical features of the character and then suggest some changes that would make the creature for example more frightening, less human, more suitable to be the hero in a story etc.

Tip Using the Merlin technique (page 80) might throw up some further ideas.

Vampire lore

In the same way that the vampire itself has evolved over time, so its strengths and weaknesses have changed to meet the demands of various plots. Here are some aspects of vampire lore, which might give children ideas for writing a vampire tale of their own, should you or they so choose. Again, ask children to 'ring the changes' by altering some items or adding more of their own. Again, the Merlin technique (page 80) might prompt further ideas.

- Vampires exist in a limbo state between life and death. In many stories, they are said to be 'undead'.
- They maintain their existence by drinking the blood of their victims, using sharp fangs which in many cases seem to be retractable like a cat's claws.
- Vampires can only walk the earth at night (though 'daywalking' creatures have recently begun to appear in books and films). Traditionally, sunlight will destroy a vampire.

- They can shapeshift into wolves, bats or fog. They cast no reflection in mirrors, polished metals or water and do not appear in photographs or video footage.
- Vampires have extreme levels of strength and speed, and some are said to be able to fly.
- An amazing power some vampires have is to control the weather, summoning a concealing fog or even a storm.
- They can entrance victims with their mesmerising gaze. However, vampires cannot cross the threshold of a building for the first time without being invited.
- During the day vampires must rest on their native soil in their own coffins.
- Ordinarily vampires are immortal and do not appear to age. A victim who dies of a vampire bite will in turn become a vampire.
- They are repelled by garlic and religious symbols and can be consumed by fire. They cannot cross running water and can be killed by driving a stake through the heart.

How to make a monster

Classic monsters in Gothic fiction include vampires, werewolves, Jekyll-Hyde and Frankenstein's creature. If you wanted children to stick strictly to the Gothic, then their choice of creatures would be limited. However, you may prefer to give their imaginations freer rein, in which case these techniques might be useful –

- Counter flipping. Using a two-colour counter or coin to provide random yes or no answers to closed questions (see also page 34).
- Monster Mash-Up. Cross-matching monster traits to create a hybrid. The writer Ronald Chetwynd-Hayes used this technique in his novel *The Monster Club* (1975). His primary monsters are the vampire, the werewolf and the ghoul (an evil spirit or phantom). Cross a vampire with a werewolf to produce a werevamp; a weregoo results from crossing a werewolf with a ghoul; a werevamp crossed with a weregoo produces a shaddy; matching a werevamp with a vamgoo gives rise to a raddy, while crossing a shaddy with a raddy produces a mock, and so on.

Chetwynd-Hayes (who alas died in 2001) was described as 'The Prince of Chill', and yet he also had a mischievous sense of humour, *The Monster Club* being funny and scary in turns.

Witch   Giant Gorilla   Frankenstein Monster   Vampire Woman   Mummy

Medusa   Werewolf   Reptile Woman   Lagoon Creature   Zombie

Space to draw and write

Invite children to combine features from two of the monsters in the visuals. They can choose their characters or roll dice to select creatures at random. As well as writing/drawing a physical description, encourage children to think about their hybrid's strengths and weaknesses, behaviour, origins and lore.

Take it further

- Pick features from more than two monsters on the grid to create a more detailed hybrid.
- The 'were' in werewolf means 'man'. Children can invent to their hearts' content by thinking of werebats, wereravens, weretigers etc., though werehamsters might not be as scary.
- Research the etymology/origin of other monster names. Vampire, for instance, comes from the Hungarian *vampir*, which perhaps derives from the Turkish *uber*, meaning witch. The Frankenstein monster takes its name from Baron Victor von Frankenstein, who created the creature – note that the creature itself is not named in Mary Shelley's novel.
- In recent years, cross-matching monsters with other characters, both fictional and real, has established itself as a subgenre. For instance, we have the animated movie *The Batman vs. Dracula* (UK rated PG), the live action film *Abraham Lincoln: Vampire Hunter* (UK rated 15), and novels such as *Mrs Darcy Versus the Aliens* and *Pride and Prejudice and Zombies*. Cross-matching characters, places and events in this way, not just in horror, offers a rich source of ideas for further stories.
- Study the mythology and folklore of different cultures, which are rich in strange and fascinating creatures.
- Take it further by asking children to write a character sketch of their creature, including a physical description, 'personality' traits, strengths and weaknesses and preferred locations.
- Write some diary entries from the monster's point of view.
- Some monsters are allegorical and represent concerns or fears in society. In the same way that aspects of science fiction prompt us to think about scientific and technological issues in the real world, so the monster-as-metaphor can offer new perspectives and insights on a range of questions and problems facing the modern world.

Monsters as metaphors

Some horror stories, including the Gothic, can have the quality of a fable, offering a message or moral as well as telling a story. Some commentators feel for example that Dracula represented its original readership's fear of disease and of strangers. More recently, the vampire mirrored society's worry about the spread of AIDS. Mary Shelley's *Frankenstein* raises the issue of whether Man should ever try to play God: the story is also about responsibility and having to face the consequences of one's actions. Werewolves, as well as Edward Hyde, remind us that, as Darwin said, we stand between the animal world and the realm of the angels, with human life being one of conflict between our baser instincts and our conscience and rationality, coupled with the fear that instinct might eventually triumph.

Oscar Wilde's *The Picture of Dorian Gray* contains strong elements of the Gothic. The main protagonist, Dorian Gray, is a handsome and wealthy young Englishman who gradually descends into a life of debauchery and crime. Gray is adored by the artist Basil Hallward, who paints his portrait and considers it his best work. As Gray's life spirals downward into dissolution, it is the painting that shows the effects of Gray's excesses rather than the man himself, who seems ageless and unblemished.

While the novel itself may be too difficult for most younger readers to tackle, they will certainly understand and likely be intrigued by the central idea…

- Set up a discussion where the children are encouraged to think about the notion of a painting suffering the ill effects of a profligate life, rather than the person himself. Would they do the same thing? What if you never had to face the consequences of your actions?

Tip We recommend Gregory Stock's *The Kids' Book of Questions* (2004), which is a treasure chest of ideas around similar topics and the broader topic of morality.

- Introduce or revisit the idea of personification. What would a monster look like that personified greed or envy, anger, spite, selfishness etc.?

> **Tip** Animals are often given human qualities, such as the wisdom of the owl, the slyness of the fox, the bravery of the lion. Use animal-related similes to help children have ideas for monsters that represent these qualities.

- Use proverbs as a source of ideas for allegorical tales. These need not necessarily be Gothic, but might be SF, fantasy, thriller, romance etc. For example –
  - Anger begins with folly and ends with repentance.
  - Anger punishes itself.
  - A hand ready to hit may cause you great trouble.
  - A man in a passion rides a mad horse.
  - Fortunate is he who does not carry envy as a companion.
  - Envy shoots at others and wounds itself.
  - Greed destroys everything.
  - Lost time is never found again.

It's worth noting that the word monster derives from the Latin *monstrum*, which in turn comes from the root *monere*, 'to warn'. To be a monster is to be an omen.

Romanticism and the pathetic fallacy

Gothic fiction has strong connections to Romanticism. This was a movement in the arts and literature that developed in the late 18th century and is characterised by –

- A love of nature, of wild places, the elements and the seasons.
- A fascination with ruins and relics of the ancient past.
- Rebellion. Romantics were non-conformists who valued individuality and resisted being one of the crowd, often reflecting this in their unconventional lifestyles (see the notes on goths on page 159).
- Heroism. Romantic stories and poems were often about people who struggled against the odds and fought for their ideals.
- Sensuality, meaning 'relating to the senses'. Romantic writing is full of sensory details: sights, sounds, smells and textures.

- Seeking the sublime – a rare emotion that is a combination of terror and awe. Romantics often found this in nature, feeling humbled and uplifted by towering mountain peaks, thundering waterfalls and huge violent thunderstorms.
- The Industrial Revolution, which for Romantics was a retrograde step away from nature as factories sprang up everywhere (William Blake's 'dark satanic mills') and people moved increasingly from the countryside into the cities and towns.
- Experimentation with poetical forms. Prior to the Romantic period, poetry was very stylised and formal. Romantic/nature poets such as Wordsworth and Keats wanted to create more informal and conversational poetry using simplified language and diction.

Gothic fiction and Romanticism appeared in the mid-18th century, with both deriving inspiration from Mediaeval literature, especially in its use of castles and other fanciful settings, a heroine, a brooding 'Byronic' hero, love and sorrow as important emotional themes and the presence of magic and the supernatural. These were a reaction against the prevailing features of Neoclassicism (a revival of the classical style), with its emphasis on rationality and order. 'Wild nature' was seen as a vibrant, living thing prompting deep emotional responses. The pathetic fallacy reflects this, being a kind of personification where human emotions are attributed to the natural world. Thus, a brooding hero's mood might be mirrored in the sullen clouds, a menacing storm or, more positively, a quiet landscape in which a character sits in deep meditative thought. (Note that personification is a broader category than pathetic fallacy, insofar as personification can link *any* human characteristic to nonhuman things, not necessarily confined to the natural world.)

The term pathetic fallacy was coined by the writer John Ruskin and derives from the Latin *pathos*, meaning 'feeling', and *fallax*, meaning 'false'. This suggests that projecting human feelings onto nature is a kind of falsehood; however, the device is used to help create the atmosphere of a scene and give deeper insight into a character's inner world of thoughts and emotions.

Activity

- Introduce or revisit the idea of personification. Judge whether the children will understand the subtler concept of pathetic fallacy. Ask them to decide which of these emotions can reasonably be applied to the features of the natural world we've listed...

Clouds	Angry
Forest	Brooding
Mist	Cruel
Moorland	Gentle
Mountains	Pitiless
Night	Raging
Ocean	Sombre
River	Sullen
Sun	Threatening
Thunder	Tranquil

Many examples of pathetic fallacy are to be found in the work of the great Romantic poets. William Wordsworth, for example, in 'Lines Composed Above Tintern Abbey', writes of the joyless daylight and the gloomy woods (though this second phrase could also be a literal statement), and in 'It is a Beauteous Evening' speaks of the twilight being calm and free, while the sun is 'sinking in his tranquillity'. In 'To Autumn', John Keats describes the season as being a close bosom friend of the sun, conspiring with him to ripen the fruits ready for harvest. The poem beautifully and powerfully evokes the Romantics' celebration of nature in all its vitality.

The poetry of Thomas Hardy, writing some decades after Keats, is similarly laced with personifications and examples of pathetic fallacy. In 'The Darkling Thrush', he talks of the darkling eye of day and compares the bleak winter landscape to a corpse. In 'Autumn in King Hintock Park', he writes of how springtime deceives but later how Earth never grieves.

See also 'Romanticising' on page 128.

Tips for writing Gothic fiction

From what we've said so far in this chapter, it should be clear that Gothic fiction is a rich and sophisticated subgenre with its roots sunk deep in classic literature, both poetry and prose. On the one hand, it celebrates nature and the landscape and explores the mystery of life, yet on the other it concerns itself with darkness, death and the ephemeral nature of existence (we refer you to Hardy again for stark examples of this in 'The Division' and 'At Day-close in November').

Our aim has been to define and to some extent describe the nature of Gothic fiction – a deeper exploration is beyond the scope of this book – creating a framework of background information to support children's writing. It may be that some of them would prefer to 'keep it simple' and write a straightforward story about rampaging werewolves or vampire hunting. Perhaps others will tackle something more challenging and try to evoke a mood of mournfulness or unease through the use of the weather, the landscape and abandoned ruins. Whatever the children's aspirations, here are some further tips and a few suggestions for plots...

In summary, Gothic fiction might feature –

1. A suitable location that helps to evoke the tone and atmosphere of the story and reflect the characters' moods. Some writers advise that the setting is itself a character in a Gothic story, thereby inviting the pathetic fallacy.
2. Specific references to time: midnight, twilight, noon, Halloween, the equinoxes and solstices etc.
3. Unnatural phenomena, such as sudden violent storms, a blood-red moon, strange atmospheric effects etc.
4. Dreams, nightmares, visions, prophecies and omens.
5. Enigmatic figures, who might turn out to be evil or good.
6. A sense of mystery, eeriness, apprehension and even dread.
7. Inquisitiveness in one or more of the characters as they try and explore the mystery (which sometimes leads to unpleasant consequences).
8. An anti-hero/heroine who has a dark side and may be trying to subvert the established order in some way or otherwise 'step over the line' into forbidden realms (such as Baron Frankenstein building his creature or Henry Jekyll exploring the shadowy corners of the human psyche).

Gothic tales also frequently feature the motifs of –

9. Transience, decay, a sense of time slipping by.
10. Family secrets and ancient curses, these perhaps being linked.
11. Children who find themselves in danger. (The children can be the main protagonists, of course, and get themselves out of trouble.)
12. A ghost who might be out for revenge, or who protects in some way or, like the spirit of Alice Drablow in Susan Hill's modern Gothic novel, *A Woman in Black*, seems to personify bitterness, rage or some other dark emotion.
13. Being told as though true, à la urban myths, and/or in the form of letters, diaries or journals.

The photograph method

This is a technique for structuring descriptive writing. Children can use drawings, photographs and video clips to practise before writing descriptions based on imagined scenes. When they are confident to do this, remind them to –

● Notice as many details as possible when thoughts stream through their mind.
● Use all of the senses as they imagine: sights, sounds, textures, smells (and tastes, if applicable).

Using the illustration –

a)   Describe the whole scene in one sentence (the establishing or wide-angle shot).
b)   Imagine the scene in colour. Add a couple more sentences mentioning the colour of the sky, the mountains and the ruins.
c)   Focus on one of the characters and describe that person in a few sentences, mentioning colour of hair and clothes.
d)   Notice two or three more things in the picture that you didn't spot before and list them now.
e)   Imagine that one of the characters speaks: decide what they say first and then describe what their voice sounds like. You can mention speed

(speaking fast or slow), pitch (how high the voice sounds), volume (loud or quiet), tone (what emotion is the character expressing?).

f)   'Turn up' other sounds in the picture and list them (such as birds singing, the wind blowing, stones rattling as the characters explore).

g)   Imagine you are one of the characters. Reach out and touch something in the scene and describe its texture in a sentence. Now notice smells in the scene – dust, old rotting wood, the damp smell of the ruins.

h)   Finally, if this were a scene in a Gothic horror story, why are the characters there and what could happen next?

Story starters

- Read the class a few suitable urban legends and ask the children to write their own versions of these.
- Show the children short video clips and invite them to turn these into story extracts or complete tales. We found some suitable ones by entering 'Gothic horror animation' into the YouTube search engine.
- Use the cover blurbs from Gothic fiction books as the basis for the children's own stories. (Some of these will also highlight the overblown and sensationalist style of some of the blurbs.)
- Ask the children to turn the examples of micro writing (page 165) into longer extracts or stories.
- Offer the class a selection of titles from published stories and use these as a prompt for storymaking. For example –
'The Return of the Sorcerer'.
'The Black Stone'.
'Dweller in the Darkness'.
'Beyond the Threshold'.
'The Shadow in the Window'.
'The Horror of Marlby Woods'.
'Winged Death'.
'Children of the Pool'.
'The Door in the Wall'.
'A Lost Inheritance'.

- Finally, you can find 'plot generating' websites online (such as www.plot-generator.org.uk). These are quite good fun to try out. Our advice is to go there yourself to harvest some ideas, tweaking as necessary in terms of content and language level before passing them on to the children.

Note

1 Friend-of-a-friend (or 'FoaF') is also a device used in urban myths, which are a kind of contemporary folklore (although versions of some stories go back many decades). FoaF tales appear mysteriously; they can be bizarre, are usually intriguing and sound almost likely enough to be true. Telling urban myths to children will quickly capture their interest and, as a side benefit, can develop their listening and questioning skills.

8 General tips when teaching writing

Summary of the chapter

- Exploring the usefulness of 'scaffolding' when teaching the skill set of writing, making sure that children are challenged but not daunted when tackling projects.
- Looking at the 'process approach' to writing, rather than being driven by the writing-as-product idea.
- Modelling the writing and 'interrogating' the text. Using the story 'The Dreamstones' (referred to in the chapter on writing historical stories) as an exemplar for giving children confidence when questioning text and when improving their own work, plus helping to create a sense of both ownership of one's writing while establishing a 'community of writers' in the classroom.
- Suggesting a few alternative marking strategies.
- Offering some final guidelines for taking the writing process forward.

Scaffolding children's writing

The aim of scaffolding is to support children in their development as writers while offering appropriate challenges that move them out of their comfort zone into their 'stretch' zone (though we dislike physical metaphors in education such as stretch, push, pull or drill, this last one being one of the worst). The idea is similar to Lev Vygotsky's notion of the 'zone of proximal development', which amounts to the difference between what pupils can do without help and what they can't. The zone of proximal development (ZPD) is where a child can carry out a task with guidance, yet still retain a sense of personal achievement and ownership of the work. Too little guidance, and a child might flounder and be discouraged; too much amounts to spoon-feeding, which hinders a young writer from standing on their own feet, this being accomplished partly by learning from one's mistakes.

In this book we have tried to offer techniques and activities that adhere to the broad principle of 'flexibility within a structure'. That is to say, children are given clear how-to guidelines that will take them through a process leading to a stated outcome, but within which they have the space to generate their own ideas and make their own decisions. The various word- and story-grids you'll find through the chapters exemplify this strategy. When using the fantasy grid on page 51 for instance, children are given definite instructions about how the process works, but because the grid incorporates the random factor through dice rolls, the particular connection that a child makes between the items selected is unpredictable and will vary from child to child. Even an idea as simple us 'the dragon was chained up' amounts to a creative connection: the child has linked two previously disparate ideas. And while the result might not be original, generally speaking, it may be the first time that *particular* child has had the thought, which he conceived by himself – an undeniable achievement worthy of a moment of sincere praise.

In that sense then the materials themselves contribute to the scaffolded nature of any child's development as a writer. We have also tried to sequence the chapters and the activities within them from the simpler to the more complex and sophisticated, so that new challenges are available as children become more adept and confident. Hopefully too, the work will remain fresh and interesting as young writers move from one genre to another, to another – though the option remains for you as teacher to cherry-pick ideas from any chapter and adapt them to fit into a different genre, or in some cases to simplify them to suit less able and/or less confident children.

Another important factor in supporting children's development as writers (and as learners more generally) is to create a classroom ethos where, if only for a short time, children need not feel that they are aiming at targets (note the militaristic metaphor), that they will be judged or that they are in competition with their peers. When listening to a story, children don't feel that they are competing with classmates to listen or that their enjoyment of the tale is being assessed. If they can feel like that when writing a story, then we believe they will become more engaged and develop as effective writers more quickly.

It's worth mentioning that the word *ethos* derives from the Greek and means 'the characteristic spirit of a time or place'. The spirit within which writing is taught and learned is crucial in fulfilling children's potential as writers. Unfortunately, 'spirit' is one of those subtle influences in education that doesn't come about in any formulaic way and cannot easily be measured, except in part by noting that children are enjoying what they're doing, the energy of which will shine in their work.

The process approach

At its simplest (or maybe most simplistic), this approach advises that children become better writers by writing; learning by doing – bearing in mind the provisos that we have already mentioned above. The process needs to be ongoing, and the purposes for which children write need to be authentic. Educationally this means 'real-life learning', where children are allowed to create meaningful and useful shared outcomes that are to a greater or lesser extent related to the real world and the children's own life experiences.

While at first glance writing about rampaging robots or hunting down evil vampires might not fit easily into this definition, we ask you to consider these points that in our view make story writing an acceptable candidate for the process approach to learning –

- As the supportive and collaborative classroom ethos towards writing becomes established, many children will engage more readily with the writing, which will lead to increased confidence and a greater willingness to share the trials, tribulations and outcomes of their work and help to shape their attitude beyond the context of creative writing.
- The kinds of thinking skills and decision-making strategies that children use in planning, writing, revising and editing their work are transferable to many non-fictional forms of writing.
- Writing stories contributes to the development of children's communication skills, helping them to become more fluent, articulate and precise both in their speaking and writing. These are life skills that are useful beyond school.
- Becoming more fluent, articulate and precise in speaking and writing supports the development of clearer and more incisive thinking, and vice versa.
- The greater self-confidence and heightened self-esteem that can come about through the enjoyment and achievement of writing stories strengthens the character and has a positive influence on a child's and young adult's social skills.

In teaching the process approach, bear in mind the following –

- Maintain high expectations as far as you possibly can with regard to children's development. Expectations determine outcomes – see Rosenthal (2003) for much more on this.
- Offer opportunities for the regular experience of writing (beyond what is mandatory in the curriculum).
- 'By increments conquer'[1]. The craft of writing is a complex interweaving of skills. Introduce, practise and guide the development of these through small steps rather than by overwhelming children with a glut of rules and instructions.
- Bring authenticity to the writing experience – see our points above.
- As far as curriculum and time constraints allow, transfer story writing skills to other forms of writing and a range of audiences, as well as emphasising the importance of writing and its underpinning thinking skills in all areas of the curriculum.
- Celebrate children's (and your own) writing through regular sharing.
- Reading and writing go hand-in-hand. Enjoy both.
- Introduce different models of writing to the children, including their work, your own, the work of children from other schools and of adult writers. Somerset Maugham once said, 'There are three golden rules for writing well. Unfortunately, nobody knows what they are'. In other words, while we can guide and advise children in the craft, many will find their own individual way of developing as a writer.
- Offer writing-related activities that encourage questioning and thinking rather than children just passively following rules.
- Teach the 'mechanics' of writing in the context of meaningful writing tasks as far as the children are concerned, rather than through separate and discrete exercises (especially if they pull, push, stretch or drill).
- When marking, try to spot *patterns* of errors in children's work rather than blanket-marking surface structure errors. Also, see alternative marking strategies on page 198.
- Value it before you evaluate it. Use quick feedback and sincere praise to encourage further effort and dampen the tendency for children to become demoralised.

Quick feedback can take the form of '3PPI' – three points of praise and one area of intention to improve. Psychologically these three points of praise are powerful. Picking out one thing a child has done well might be a fluke; two things done well might be a coincidence, but finding three things done well makes it more difficult for a child to deny her achievement. They also 'cushion' comments relating an area that needs to be improved, comments that a child might otherwise take to be negative criticism. And here it's useful to point out that most if not all writers will admit that they are still learning. Someone once compared the writing process to walking along a road. Some people are farther ahead than others, but all have the same obstacles to overcome and the same fine views to enjoy.

Modelling the writing

Two useful aspects of this idea are –

- To do some writing yourself when you ask the children to write.
- To explore with the class how other writers achieve their effects.

Tackling writing tasks yourself puts you through the same experience that you've given the children. It will give you insights into what it *feels* like to write creatively; the frustrations when things are not turning out well and the pleasure and satisfaction when they are. Because writing is a process, gaining an insider's view of it offers a wealth of opportunities to share thoughts with the children and help to bind the community of writers that we mentioned earlier.

When we talk of how other writers do it, we don't mean 'how to do it' but how *they* do it, bearing in mind Somerset Maugham's comment on page 188. While there are 'standard' rules, guidelines and pieces of advice for improving writing, ultimately every writer evolves a personal style and working method.

The writer and educationist Pie Corbett suggests that improving writing follows the 'imitate, innovate, invent' route. Many children will have favourite writers, so there's an opportunity here to allow them to use the characters, settings, plot elements and style of a favourite author in their own work. They can imitate to their hearts' content until they begin to develop their own individual 'voice'. You can also help children to look at the work of other writers with a more analytical eye, drawing out the techniques and strategies that authors use to make an impact. Encouraging children to try these out for themselves broadens their experience and makes them more discerning about what would work in their own writing.

Children often seem to think that you need to be 'clever' to be a writer. Our response is that it's more important to be 'nosy'; that is, by noticing things and by asking questions. A useful first step in modelling the writing of others, therefore, is to notice what they are trying to do and to ask questions about it (however naïve these appear to be). 'Interrogating' a text means to read it closely and critically which, however, should not be at the expense of reading a piece for pleasure.

In the chapter on writing a historical story, we used 'The Dreamstones' as an exemplar to support the children's writing activities. The annotated text offers some advice on the decisions we made in the planning and during the actual writing. If you decide to show this to the children, invite them to ask any questions that come to mind. Examples we've encountered about the opening of the story include –

- Where does the word 'Samhain' come from?
- What does Corieltauvi mean?
- Is the story set in Britain? Did wolves really live in Britain?
- What gods did these people worship?
- What does 'sacred' mean?
- What was the point of sacrificing animals to the gods? Did the people eat the animals afterwards?

Not all of these questions are answered in the story, and some children might feel that this is a failing. Point out that writers try to ensure that everything in a story is there (or not there) for a good reason that hopefully makes the story better. So, encourage the children to reflect on *why* the story is as it is.

1. The Dreamstones.	Decide on age of readership before writing; 9–10 in this case. That will determine language level and story length.
2. The tribe had been getting ready for the celebration for days. It was the great festival of Samhain. It marked the end of summer and the start of long cold winter months. The people of the tribe – the Corieltauvi – dwelt in a small settlement in a narrow valley. One day this place would be called Hallaton. It was where a boy named Weland and his family lived.	Setting the scene in terms of time and place. Factual details increase believability.

Introduce a main character early on. |

3. Weland was thirteen years old. His father Brennus had sent him out on to the hills to herd the sheep. As Samhain drew closer and bad weather was due, the animals had to be brought closer to where the people lived. Wolves roamed the countryside and were especially hungry, and therefore bold, in the wintertime.	Child protagonists are often two or three years older than the age of the reader. Anticipation of danger helps to create tension.
4. The pigs, sheep and cattle that would not be used for breeding were sacrificed to the gods. This happened at a special shrine or sacred place that had been built on the hill. A wooden fence partly circled the shrine. In the very centre was a great block of wood. Here the animals were killed as offerings. But people also left little statues, coins and other gifts here too.	Language is intentionally plain and simple. Sentences are relatively short.
*	After setting the scene, the narrative focuses on the hero of the story.
5. Weland sighed to himself. He was not very good at herding sheep. Even the few that he'd found hurried away from him instead of being guided by his stick. Besides, he was too busy thinking of Bettrys, who he thought was the prettiest girl of the whole clan. She was tall and fair and her smile made Weland's breath catch. He hoped that when she was old enough she would choose him to marry… But she might pick Ambior instead. This was Weland's great rival, and son of Ariovis who was a very important Druid priest. Only Vepomaros, the chieftain of the clan, had more authority.	Creating conflict by introducing Ambior – a 'character triangle'. Descriptive details can be 'sprinkled' through the story. Not all characters need to be described when they are first mentioned. Mention of the tribe's religion creates a sense of 'otherness'.
6. Weland was lost in these thoughts when someone barged into him and knocked him to the ground. He looked up in time to see Ambior stride by – herding at least ten sheep, and with a cruel smile on his face. 'Watch where you're going, cow pat!' Ambior sneered.	Rivalry with Ambior is one of the problems in the story that needs to be resolved.
7. Weland sighed for a second time. Ambior would get all the credit for the herding while Weland would have to explain why *he* came home empty handed… Unless he could find some stray sheep in the woodland further up the hill.	
8. It was his last hope, so he hurried and soon found himself among the trees. After a short while he stopped to listen for any sheep – but instead he heard the slow gentle clump of horses' hooves and the voices of men close by	Increasing the tension further. First mention of a larger problem and further anticipation of danger.

9. Weland's heart leapt. What if they were Roman soldiers coming to attack the settlement! He had to warn everyone! He turned to retrace his steps – only to be pinned to a tree by a powerful arm. Weland found himself staring into the fiercest eyes he had ever seen.	The en-dash is used to change the focus of the sentence, in this case the sudden appearance of the fierce man.
10. 'So Little Hare, are you going to run or freeze!' Although the man looked frightening – he had long white hair washed with lime and a drooping white moustache – his voice sounded mischievous and playful. 'Because the wolf will catch you anyway!'	After the tension, some light relief.
11. 'But he won't make Little Hare squeal!' Weland spoke out defiantly and he could see that the stranger was pleased.	Dialogue causes the reader's eyes to scan the page more quickly, increasing the story's pace.
12. 'Good answer, young sir'. The man let him go and ruffled his hair. 'My name is Carad. I have travelled here with my friends Aisling and Braeden. And who are you?'	
13. 'I am Weland, son of Brennus'.	
14. 'Is he your chieftain?'	Anticipating moving the plot forward.
15. 'No sir, that is Vepomaros'.	
16. 'Then please take me to him, for I have important matters to discuss'. *	Jumping straight into Carad's account also helps to make the narrative pacier. Establishing the Romans as the antagonists.
17. 'The Romans could not surround us because we had taken our stand on the hill. There was woodlandbehind us and marshland in front. The Roman cavalry charged but our spears rained down and they could not break our ranks. And when their infantrymen marched against us, our war chariots swept in from the sides – each one bearing a warrior standing astride the paired horses – and cut through their lines again and again!'	
18. Vepomaros, Brennus and other men of the settlement listened closely as Carad told his story. Weland found it all very exciting. But he saw that nearby Ambior stood with the usual sneer on his face, while his father Ariovis looked very suspicious.	Using authentic rather than invented names makes the story more believable.
19. 'So, Carad', he said in a challenging tone, 'you tell us the Silurian tribe of Cymru stood up stoutly to the Roman attack?'	

20. 'Many tribesmen fought bravely and well!'	
21. 'And yet I have heard that the Silures were beaten on their own ground and routed. This was because the Romans fought as one trained force, while the Silures were a disorganised rabble'.	
22. Even Weland could see that Ariovis was trying to provoke Carad. He thought this was very ill mannered, since Carad and his friends were guests of the clan. Whatever Carad's reply might have been, he was interrupted by Bettrys who stepped forward to offer him more ale. Weland smiled, knowing she had picked her moment well and, once again, showed wisdom beyond her years.	It's fine for characters to express opinions, but the author should not inject their own opinions into the story.
23. 'I also heard', Ariovis went on, 'that a man who fought with the Silures and was an inspiration to them – a man named Caratacus – was forced to flee; and his brother, wife and daughters were captured. No doubt many Romans will be looking for him…'	Building tension further with Ariovis's implied threat.
24. Carad ignored the priest and spoke to the whole assembly. 'Fellow Britons, I tell you these stories to warn you that the Romans have not come here to form friendships. They want only to conquer and to plunder our beautiful land. I say again that if the Silurians were beaten in this battle they will not lose the greater war against the invaders. They struggle to keep a way of life that the Romans would steal from us. I urge you to follow the Silures' example and fight – fight like the wolf rather than bowing down like sheep!'	There is ambiguity here as to whether Carad is a troublemaker.
25. These were stirring words and Weland felt flushed with pride to be a Briton. The people who had listened to Carad began to talk among themselves. Vepomaros felt that time was needed to reflect on what Carad had said, and so he ordered that the feasting should begin.	
26. Low wooden tables were brought and set near the bonfires where the crowd had been sitting. Hay was scattered on the ground for greater comfort. According to tradition guests should eat first: Carad, Aisling, Braeden and the other visiting clansmen were each offered the roasted right forelimb of a pig. These animals had been sacrificed earlier to the god Moccus, who was a protector god of hunters. It was considered good manners to eat all of the meat on the joint, which Carad and his friends did gladly since they were very hungry.	A few details about the culture add colour to the story.

27. Afterwards more food, the fruits of the harvest, appeared and everyone was urged to eat their fill. Even though the mood earlier had been serious, as the evening wore on and the moon rose bright and full, the atmosphere became one of celebration. People thanked the gods for helping the tribe to flourish.	Mention of the gods adds a touch of the exotic and anticipates the mysticism that will follow.
28. Weland had chosen to sit close to Bettrys. He couldn't wait any longer to find out how she felt about him. Before he arrived he expected to find Ambior there, but Weland's rival was nowhere to be seen. So it was that he enjoyed eating with Bettrys, though he felt too nervous to ask her about the future. He tried instead to be light-hearted and make jokes. And although Bettrys laughed Weland realised that she was troubled about something.	Ambior's absence and Bettrys's concerns foreshadow the unfolding of the story's main problem
29. 'What is it?' he asked at last. 'I know you are concerned. Would you rather I went away?'	
30. Bettrys frowned, then smiled at him. 'Oh Weland no, it's not you. I have a feeling that something is terribly wrong, but I don't know quite what'.	
31. Weland did not doubt her words for an instant. While the priests of the tribe were men, a number of the women, including Bettrys, had the gift of future sight. And while the women's visions were not always clear, they were rarely wrong.	The sense of mysticism, introduced earlier by mention of the gods, is now heightened by what we are told about Bettrys.
32. 'Then why don't you go to the shrine and ask the gods for guidance?' Weland said. 'I will come with you'.	
33. So they walked along the moonlit path together. Other people from the tribe, in pairs and small groups, were visiting the shrine also but only one or two people at a time went up to the altar block to worship.	Mentioning the moonlight adds to the drama and romance of the scene.
34. When it was their turn, Weland placed a coin in a pit beside the entrance. It was a silver piece that Vepomaros had given him, showing a horse and letters that Weland couldn't understand. But it was beautiful even so. It was a tradition that the chieftain gave each member of the clan a coin to offer to the gods. Weland respected this, but would love to have kept the shiny coin for himself.	

35. Bettrys went to the altar and knelt before it, gazing at a small wooden statue that had startling eyes of blue glass. She knelt in silence, then stood and walked quickly back to Weland. He could see that her eyes were full of shadows and darkness.	Vivid details should be used sparingly.
36. '*I know*', she whispered with a trembling voice. 'I have seen. Ariovis intends to betray Carad and his men to the Romans. He has sent word to the garrison at Ratae… I don't know how long ago that was, but some time tonight Roman soldiers will come and try to capture Carad, or even kill him –'	The story's main problem is revealed.
37. 'Then we must warn him!'	
38. 'Wait, Weland wait!' Bettrys gripped his arm. 'There is something I must do first. Come with me quickly'.	Not revealing Bettrys's intention yet increases the tension.
39. Instead of going towards the village, Bettrys led Weland farther up the hill to an outcrop of rock, where a spring bubbled out of a cleft. Bettrys dropped to her knees and selected three stones from among the hundreds that lay in the water.	
40. 'I lift these stones for courage, freedom and right action'. She placed two in a pouch tied at her waist. 'One is for Carad, one is for me'. And she handed Weland the third. 'May they stay with us until our journey's end. They are dreamstones', she explained. 'And they help us to walk the right path in life'. She smiled fondly upon him and Weland's heart soared.	The mystical nature of the dreamstones is more believable following earlier mention of the gods and the women's future sight.
41. 'I will go and warn Carad', she said. 'Will you head towards Ratae, and at the first sign of soldiers approaching hurry back to tell us?'	
42. 'I will do that', Weland promised. 'Stay safe Bettrys'. She nodded and then with a flicker of long golden hair and a light pattering of footsteps she was gone. * 	
43. Weland took the high ridge way heading west towards Ratae, 'the place of ramparts'. It was rumoured that the Romans were building defences there before advancing to the north, into the territory of the Brigantes tribe. From his high viewpoint Weland could see the glow of fires from the garrison, even though it was still miles away.	More factual details.

44. He continued moving at a brisk pace, seeing his way by moonlight. His eyes grew used to the silvery landscape as he gazed down into the valley. His attention was fixed there, so it was that he failed to notice what was right in front of him until it was too late.

45. A powerful blow struck the side of his head and smashed him to the ground. 'You're not even fit to herd sheep', said a familiar voice. Ambior's strong hands grabbed Weland's tunic and dragged him up, only to batter him down again with two more mighty punches.

46. As Weland lay dazed he heard the heavy clumping of horses and was aware of two or three cavalrymen riding past. Ambior was already returning to the settlement with the Romans. Weland had failed in his mission. *Although*, he thought, *I could still get there ahead of them by going through the woods. If only…*

47. Ambior started to haul Weland to his feet for a third time. But Weland was expecting this and swung a solid right fist into Ambior's face. Weland thought he would need to fight hard for victory, but with a soft grunt Ambior simply fell and lay still, quite unconscious.

48. Weland chuckled as he realised why – he still held the dreamstone in his hand and it had added weight to his blow.

Shorter paragraphs increase pace. There is also some artistic licence here, as Weland could easily have broken fingers by lashing out with the stone in his hand.

49. For a moment he thought his troubles were over, but then to his dismay he saw one of the Roman horsemen turn and begin cantering back. The soldier drew his short stabbing sword as he came.

50. Weland started to panic. He wanted to run, but fear kept him frozen to the spot. Then he remembered what Carad had said. Do not die like sheep. Fight like the wolf. And those words gave him strength as a wild idea leapt into his mind.

51. Without a second thought Weland hurled the dreamstone at the Roman horseman and quite by luck (though he would never admit that!) it struck the soldier squarely on his unprotected forehead. He tumbled from his horse and crashed to the ground.

52. Weland grabbed the soldier's silver parade helmet and also took his sword, thinking the other horsemen might return. But they had moved out of sight and earshot and galloped on ahead.	
53. But now there was no time to lose. Weland ran as fast as he could along the ridge and then down into the woods towards the village.	
*	
54. It was an hour later. Nearby among the trees Aisling and Braeden waited with the horses. Vepomaros, Carad, Bettrys and Weland were gathered beside the shrine while Ariovis at Vepomaros' command stood nervously beyond the fence. Weland's story, with the Roman helmet and sword to prove it, could not be denied: the priest had brought disgrace upon himself, although through Carad's forgiveness not to the tribe itself.	The denouement, where plot threads are drawn together and matters are finally resolved.
55. 'We are grateful to you Carad', Vepomaros said with a bow, then smiled at the children. 'And to you also, for if it had not been for your quick action, the soldiers would have found you. More may come here later, but I have Ariovis and his son's promise of silence. You will not be followed, Carad. And now I will leave you three to make your farewells'.	
56. So it was that they said their goodbyes. Bettrys placed the dreamstone delicately into Carad's hand as she explained its purpose. Likewise Carad gave his blessing of good fortune, then he slipped a golden ring from his little finger and slid it onto Bettrys' right thumb (since her other fingers were all too small!)	
57. 'And for you Weland, who has brought such honour to your family…' He took a gold torc from his neck and placed it around Weland's, whose eyes filled with tears of gratitude and pride.	
58. 'But where will you go now?' Weland wondered.	
59. 'I travel north, to the land of the Brigantes, ahead of the Romans. There I hope to win their queen, Cartimandua, to my way of thinking. Whether I succeed or not, the gods only know. But I must try: for in future times the people will look upon the labour of the Romans and call it the work of the giants. But by then they will be nothing but ghosts. I do not wish to see the Britons become ghosts before them, dying like sheep by their hand'.	Opportunity here for a sequel.

60. With a final firm clasp of Weland's shoulder, Carad turned and vanished among the trees leaving the two youngsters by themselves.	
61. 'There could still be trouble in store for us', Bettrys said softly, though with no fear in her voice now. *And greater trouble*, Weland thought, *since I have lost the dreamstone she gave me!*	
62. But at that, somehow knowing what was going through his mind, Bettrys simply chuckled and clasped his fingers and said, 'You are not to worry Weland. We will go looking for the dreamstone tomorrow'.	
63. So they did – and of course, Bettrys knew exactly where it lay.	Hints that a greater friendship will develop.

Take it further by –

● Asking children from time to time to annotate their own texts, making notes on why they did what they did, and how they might do things differently if they could. To facilitate this, suggest that they write the story on the left-hand page of their books and put their notes/annotations/questions on the right. They can also use the right-hand page for changes of mind.

● Invite children to make up comprehension questions for their own stories and those of their classmates. This creates the opportunity for children to reflect critically on their own and others' work.

Suggestions for alternative marking strategies

● Patterns of errors (see page 188) sometimes indicate emergent under-standing. Children are still learning; they are on their way to a fuller under-standing of how writing works. For instance, one child asked us, 'How many books have you writed?' Her teacher pointed out that she should have said 'written', which is correct; but obviously the girl had some understanding of the past tense. Recognising this and giving credit for it is at least as impor-tant as correcting the technical error. Similarly, when a new aspect of the mechanics of writing is introduced, some children will 'over-apply' the rule at first, taking a scattergun approach with apostrophes for example and putting one before and/or after every word ending with 's'. Again, this is evidence of emergent understanding, and as teachers, we might wonder if correcting every misplaced apostrophe is the most effective way of helping children to learn.

- Selective marking. Rather than marking every aspect of a piece of work, pick out one or two and tell the children beforehand that today you will just be checking for apostrophes or 'strong' verbs, or you will just be reading for pleasure and the only marking you do will be a comment at the end to say what you enjoyed about the story (or you might use the 3PPI tactic). Selective marking not only saves valuable time, but children are more likely to read and absorb what you've written: blanket-marking work might deter children from reflecting on your comments and carries the real danger that the message you convey is 'look at all this stuff you've got wrong', leading to disillusionment and a sense of failure.

- Alternative marking signs. A range of traditional marking signs already exists in schools, and these tend mainly to flag up errors and suggest corrections. They can be complemented by other signs that highlight the thinking the children have done as part of the writing process. Here are some of our ideas, though of course you and the children could think of more. As well as using them yourself, suggest to the children that they too can use them to indicate to you that they have understood and decided to incorporate particular aspects of writing into their work. If that's the case, a simple tick or 'good' is sufficient to acknowledge the pupil's efforts. Point out to the children that they won't be expected to feature all of these aspects of writing in every story. It's important that young writers don't feel overwhelmed by things to remember. On the other hand, some of the items on the list must feature in certain genres – thriller must have pace and tension, Gothic horror stories benefit from atmosphere and vivid description of place etc.

 A⃗	Action
 ⬭	Atmosphere
⸙B	Backstory
B̆	Believability
Cḃ	Character Development
⟨M	Character Motivation
�F⌃	Foreshadowing
⦾⦾	Mix of Genres
VM	Vivid Metaphor
⋀	Use of Motifs
 ☆	Multisensory writing
 ⊘	Original
D̲	Description of place
 P⃗	Pace
 ⌄⃗	Use of Subplot
 �	Use of Tension

Tip One or two of the signs feature a positive value judgement – Vivid Metaphor and Original and Use of Motifs with a tick incorporated into the signs. The others are 'neutral' and simply acknowledge the aspect of narrative that you've spotted. You can, of course, augment the signs with a tick or 'good', or give advice such as 'description of place needed' or 'look again at pace here'.

Some further guidelines

Finally, and by way of summarising the points we've made, here are some further tips that we hope will support your own and the children's development as writers.

1. Mistakes are not only inevitable, they're positively beneficial insofar as they build resilience, a willingness to learn and the recognition that learning never ends. Apparently, the inventor and entrepreneur James Dyson created over 5,000 prototypes of his innovative vacuum cleaner before he got it right, admitting that he learned something from each failure.

2. Writing is hard and does not come naturally. As we've said, it's a complex interweaving of many skills that takes time even to begin to master. It's not the same as learning to speak – bring up babies and young children in a rich language environment and they will learn to speak fluently and articulately. In that sense, it 'happens by itself'. Learning writing is a more artificial process that requires determination and perseverance as well as a degree of knowledge.

3. Writing regularly gets you there. There's enormous pressure to 'cover' the curriculum in the time given, and it's easy for some subjects and learning experiences to become marginalised. But as we've said, the skills that children learn when writing prose fiction are directly applicable to other written forms and enhance children's ability to communicate well more generally. Regular practice is the quickest route to improvement (this is surely a truism?), so we urge you to find time for regular story-writing sessions.

4. Reading, talking and writing go hand-in-hand (if you'll allow us three hands). A collaborative approach within a community of writers powerfully supports children's progress, especially if it's built into school policy and doesn't rely on the efforts of individual teachers going it alone.

5. The most effective writers are independent as well as creative thinkers. Advice about how to write well abounds, but ultimately children as they become young adults will need to work out their own best working methods. Well, that's our advice anyway.

6. Writing improves bit by bit over time, by putting one word in front of another. It's misguided to expect children to have absorbed all of your teaching about spelling, punctuation and grammar and many other aspects of

writing as they tackle their latest piece. A useful analogy is that knowing the names of the different parts of my car's engine doesn't necessarily make me a better driver.

7.   Maintain high expectations for your children's achievements and encourage them to have faith in their own imaginations. All of the children in the class can come up with ideas to write about, especially if they have a toolbox of how-to techniques.

8.   Writing is rewriting. It's not often that a story or other piece of writing comes out right the first time. The process approach wisely advocates that the road to writing well follows the steps of prewriting/planning – drafting – revising – editing – publishing.

Having ideas is often the easy part of the writing process. Finding the words to express them is more difficult, and it's hard work (though need be no less enjoyable for that). Once the first draft is done, encourage the children to consider (after a period of 'cooling off' time, a few days at least) what changes they could make to improve the work. This need not mean a complete redraft – which many children dislike doing – but might amount to some annotations on the right-hand page of their writing books. Revising is more to do with the narrative content of the story, whereas editing focuses more on stylistic and grammatical aspects of the work once a child has a draft that they are happy with. Publishing means 'making the work public', which in a school context can mean sharing it with classmates, organising story sharing sessions with other classes and staging the occasional celebration to which parents and governors are invited. Some schools also undertake publishing projects where children's work sees print in books – something that's much easier to do these days in-house or through self-publishing companies and print-on-demand facilities.

9.   In the end, technical accuracy matters. The aim of most writing is to communicate effectively, and that involves accurate spelling, punctuation and grammar. The process approach offers a rigorous and effective strategy for refining and polishing a piece of work so that it's the best it can be. As and when you think the time is right, point out to pupils that one day they'll likely write a letter of application for a job or need to compose some equally important piece of writing. How accurately they say it is as important as what they say: correct spelling and punctuation feed into the overall impression the reader forms, which can have important consequences.

10. As the philosopher Alain De Botton says in his book *The News: A User's Manual* (De Botton, 2014), developing as a writer means paying attention to language, picking out 'animating details' and keeping control of pace and structure. Make it clear to children that in this endeavour, no words are ever wasted. Every word a child writes is another step along the road to becoming a better writer.

Enjoy the journey.

Note

1 This advice comes from the educationalist Will Ord in the context of teaching children to do philosophical enquiry, but it's equally applicable here.

Story steps – vocabulary

Allegory – A story or other art form that contains an implicit message, often political or moral. The characters and events in an allegorical story represent or symbolise ideas or issues relevant to human life. An allegory can also be thought of as an extended metaphor, and an example of a story that is not true, but which *tells you something true*.

Brainstorming – This is a thinking technique for generating ideas within a group or with a partner. A useful maxim to keep in mind is 'How many ideas can we have and what use can we make of them?' Brainstorming applies to the first part of that advice. An initial stimulus is used to 'kickstart' the imagination. As ideas appear spontaneously, they are recorded, but no analysis of them or judgements about them are made at this point. The sole aim is to create as many ideas as possible. Analysis of usefulness comes later.

Characters – The word has a complicated history, originally coming from the Greek *kharaktēr*, meaning 'a stamping tool'. From there the term evolved through Latin and Middle English to take on the sense of 'a distinctive mark' and subsequently a feature or trait, leading then to the more modern notion of a description of a person's distinguishing features. When writing short stories, children should be encouraged to describe main characters using a few vivid details rather than attempting long and involved descriptions. In longer pieces of work or in a sequence of stories featuring the same character, further details can be added. Characters reveal their personalities and motivations through dialogue, action, facial expressions and body language, plus of course the inclusion of descriptive details of physical appearance.

Companion – Literally in Old French a companion is someone who 'breaks bread with another'. Both the hero and villain in a story may have a companion or sidekick whose function is often more than just to act as a sounding board for the main character's views, plans etc. A companion can highlight faults or redeeming features in the hero/villain, modify the main character's actions, serve as comic relief if the story calls for it, and have a history and motivations of their own. Thus, a companion in this sense is greater than a mere underling or passive follower.

Dialogue – This means a conversation between two or more characters. Dialogue is an important part of most stories for the following reasons –

- It moves the plot forward.
- It reveals more of the characters' personalities.
- It lets the reader know characters' reactions to other people, places and situations.

Dialogue breaks up blocks of narrative. The reader's eye moves more quickly down the page so the story flows by more quickly.

When using dialogue, it's important that the reader can keep track of who is speaking, and to whom. 'Said' is the most commonly used tag to identify who's talking. You have probably told the class to vary the story by using other verbs such as commented, pointed out, shouted, yelled and so on. Also 'ly' adverbs, for example, pointed out impatiently, shouted angrily, yelled hysterically etc. This is fine, but also advise the children not to overdo it by trying to use a different verb and adverb every time a character speaks.

Tip Encourage children when reading a story to notice how the author allows the reader to keep track of who is speaking.

Genre – A style or category in art, music and literature. In literature, the term 'genre fiction' or 'popular fiction' is used to distinguish it from literary fiction. In genre-based stories, a number of conventional characters, settings, objects and plot devices tend to appear. In terms of children's writing, familiarising them with the conventions of a genre gives them a structure within which they can work. Knowing the conventions allows more experienced young writers to use them *un*conventionally, i.e. in more original ways. See also 'Sub-genre'.

Hero – The hero is a major character type in stories. Originally the term carried connotations of 'a demi-god', and this still applies when writing about superheroes. In more down to earth stories, the hero is made more believable by showing human weaknesses, as well as traits such as kindness, compassion and loyalty. However, if a hero is portrayed with a character flaw and/or a 'dark side' they become more interesting. The primary function of the hero is to resolve problems created by the primary villain and so restore balance and harmony to the world.

Horror – As a fictional genre, the aim of horror is to scare readers/viewers, create a sense of tension, unease, 'chill', menace, shock or dread and (though this might not be appropriate for young writers) revulsion or disgust. If we think of the horror genre as a tree, then it has numerous sub-genre branches, including ghost stories, vampire tales, werewolves, Gothic and many more, each with their own conventions and motifs.

Morality tale – Similar to a parable insofar as such stories aim to highlight differences between good and evil, and possible consequences that can follow from such actions.

Nanotechnology – Technology that deals with the very small. A pioneering work on micro-machines and their applications is *Unbounding the Future* (1992) by Eric Drexler, Chris Peterson and Gayle Pergamit. This was first published in the early 1990s when nanotechnology was in its infancy. Now, nanotech is a reality taking many different forms, and 'nanites' have become a familiar trope in SF stories.

Paganism – A non-Christian or pre-Christian religion outside of the world's main religions, incorporating nature worship.

Parable – A story that aims to teach a moral or spiritual lesson.

Personification – Attributing human qualities and attributes to non-human creatures and inanimate things.

Polytheism – Belief in and the worshipping of more than one god.

Prophecy – A prediction of what will happen in the future. In the day-to-day world, this might be based on reasoning and inference. In stories, prophecies are often made by supernatural means, and so feature often in Gothic horror.

Protagonist – A main character in a story, usually the hero, usually pitted against the antagonist or villain. The term 'protagonist' comes from Greek drama and means the person who led the chorus.

Recounting – This is the passing on of events (for our purposes, of a story) in chronological order, using the text as reference.

Retelling – This is the passing on of events of a story using one's memory. A retelling may incorporate the extra skills of summarising and embellishing.

Stooge – A character that is the butt of others' often malicious humour, or someone forced to do routine or unpleasant work.

Subgenre – A sub-category of a larger genre in literature, film, music etc.

Supernatural fiction – Stories that in a variety of ways contradict the way we think the material world works. Many though not all horror stories rely on supernatural themes, characters and plot devices.

Synonym – Words or phrases that mean almost the same thing. 'Large' and 'big' are said to be synonymous. The word itself comes from the Greek meaning 'with' and 'name', though we usually think of it as 'same name'.

Third person – Refers to the style of writing about characters as an outsider looking in at the world of the story. So, we write *about* the hero, villain, companion etc. The value of third person writing is that the author can 'jump about' in time and space, from character to character, from scene to scene. Care must be taken though that an author doesn't impose their own views on the narrative. This is called narrative or authorial intrusion and happens when the writer addresses the reader directly or projects themself into the fictional world.

Vengeance – Punishment given for wrongdoing and injustice, often accompanied by strong emotions of anger, grief etc.

Vignette – A short vivid description or episode.

Villain – The function of the principal villain in a story is to create discord, chaos, fear etc. through evil and selfish motives. Originally the word meant a peasant or miser but has evolved to mean a scoundrel or criminal. In the same way that a completely good hero is not a believable character, so a totally evil villain stretches credulity and remains a character that is cold, detached and with whom the reader finds it hard to identify. A more interesting and believable villain will have some redeeming feature (or at least a human backstory) and may even be portrayed as a lovable rogue.

Visualise – To form a mental image. Although the term suggests imagining pictures, encouraging children to imagine sounds, textures, smells and tastes means that more multisensory references will appear in their work. This is an aspect of 'metacognition', the potential we all have for noticing and manipulating our thoughts.

Vocabulary – The word itself comes from the Latin for 'word' or 'name' and, applied to an individual, refers to the number of words that person knows. Words that someone uses in speaking and writing constitute the active vocabulary, while words that someone understands but rarely uses form their passive vocabulary. Enriching children's vocabulary generally and more specifically across different subject areas is a primary aim of education. In terms of creative writing, caution must be used and a balance must be struck: children should not be encouraged to grab at the first word that comes to mind, as this can lead to cliché and 'tired' writing. On the other hand, advising children to pepper their work with more unusual terms can give the writing a 'forced' and artificial feel. As children develop, of course, most of them will learn to become more discriminating in picking the right words for the job in hand.

Story steps checklist

	Ghost story	Fantasy	Science fiction	Historical	Pirate adventure	Thriller	Gothic horror	Writing tips
Adjectives	✓		✓				✓	
Age range				✓				
Anachronism				✓	✓			
Anagrams					✓			
Anti-hero							✓	
Artful vagueness					✓		✓	
Artistic licence				✓				
Aspects of a story	✓		✓					
Association web			✓					
Atmosphere	✓						✓	
Backstory				✓				
Because game				✓				
Believability			✓					
Careering						✓		
Characters	✓	✓	✓					
Character grid						✓		
Character names			✓					
Character traits					✓			
Character types							✓	
Character web						✓		
Character wheel					✓			
Cliché		✓						
Cliffhangers						✓		
Coin flip game		✓				✓		
Comprehension				✓				
Conflict			✓	✓				
Confrontation						✓		
Critiquing work				✓				
Decision-making			✓	✓				
Description of place	✓		✓				✓	
Dialogue	✓							
Dilemmas						✓		
Editing								✓
Emotions, naming	✓							
Ethos of writing								✓
Etymology		✓	✓		✓			
Free writing				✓				
Flashback				✓				
Flash fiction							✓	

	1	2	3	4	5	6	7	8
Focus in writing						✓		
Foreshadowing				✓				
Generalisations		✓						
Genre switching		✓			✓			
Hooks						✓		
Hyperbole							✓	
Idioms					✓			
If-then thinking					✓			
Improving work				✓				
Logical consistency			✓					
Marking strategies								✓
Maybe thinking						✓		
Meanwhile game				✓				
Merlin technique			✓	✓				
Metaphors				✓	✓		✓	
Minor characters					✓			
Modelling writing	✓							✓
Morality							✓	
Motifs/tropes	✓	✓	✓		✓		✓	
Motivation						✓		
Narrative elements		✓						
Narrative template		✓						
Naming characters			✓					
Originality		✓						
Overwriting				✓				
Pathetic fallacy							✓	
Personification	✓		✓				✓	
Planning				✓				
Plot	✓		✓					
Point of view	✓			✓				
Prefixes		✓	✓					
Prequel				✓				
Process approach								✓
Proofreading								✓
Proverbs		✓					✓	
Questions, kinds of				✓	✓			
Randomness						✓	✓	
Research				✓	✓			
Romanticizing					✓			
Romanticism							✓	
Scaffolding								✓
Seed stories		✓						
Sequel				✓				
Settings	✓	✓	✓				✓	
Shout lines						✓		
Show, don't tell						✓		
Speculation					✓			
Stereotypes		✓			✓		✓	
Story grid				✓	✓			
Story line planner	✓				✓			
Story starters	✓						✓	
Story threads		✓						
Strength of reasons			✓					

(Continued)

	Ghost story	Fantasy	Science fiction	Historical	Pirate adventure	Thriller	Gothic horror	Writing tips
Structure and function			✓					
Sub-elements			✓					
Subgenres		✓	✓					
Subplots						✓		
Technobabble			✓					
Themes		✓	✓					
Third person	✓			✓				
Thumbnail overview			✓					
Timelines				✓				
Time span				✓				
Titles for stories			✓					
Tropes (motifs)					✓			
12-panel game						✓		
Unpredictability						✓		
Urban myths							✓	✓
Verbs			✓					
Visual planning	✓				✓			
Vivid details			✓					
What happens next						✓		
What if?			✓					
Word box			✓			✓		
Word cloud			✓					
Wordplay			✓					
Word search					✓			

References and resources

De Botton, A. *The News: A User's Manual.* London: Hamish Hamilton, 2014.

Bowkett, S. *Countdown to Creative Writing.* Abingdon, Oxon: Routledge, 2009.

Bowkett, S. *Developing Literacy and Creative Writing Through Storymaking.* Maidenhead: Open University Press – McGraw-Hill House, 2010.

Bowkett, S. *A Creative Approach to Teaching Writing.* London: Bloomsbury, 2014.

Bowkett, S. *Jumpstart! Thinking Skills and Problem Solving.* Abingdon, Oxon: Routledge, 2015.

Bowkett, S. *Developing Self-Confidence in Young Writers.* London: Bloomsbury, 2017. (pp. 24–27).

Bowkett, S. *Jumpstart! Philosophy in the Classroom.* Abingdon, Oxon: Routledge, 2018.

Brunvand, J. H. *The Vanishing Hitchhiker: Urban Legends and Their Meanings.* London: Pan Books, 1981.

Brunvand, J. H. *Curses! Broiled Again!* New York: Norton, 1989.

Brunvand, J. H. *The Baby Train.* New York: Norton, 1993.

Buckley, J. *Pocket P4C: Getting Started with Philosophy for Children.* Chelmsford: One Slice Books, 2011.

Chetwynd-Hayes, R. *The Monster Club.* London: New English Library, 1975.

Clarke, A. C. *Profiles of the Future: An Inquiry into the Limits of the Possible.* London: Phoenix, 2000.

Drexler, E., Peterson, C. & Pergamit, G. *Unbounding the Future: The Nanotechnology Revolution.* London: Simon & Schuster, 1992.

Egan, K. *The Educated Mind: How Cognitive Tools Shape Our Understanding.* Chicago: University of Chicago Press, 1997.

Fisher, R. *Teaching Thinking.* London: Continuum, 2004.

Garner, A. *Elidor.* Harmondsworth, Middlesex: Penguin, 1972.

Goss, M. *The Evidence for Phantom Hitchhikers.* Wellingborough: The Aquarian Press, 1984.

Graves, Donald H. *Writing: Teachers and Children at Work*. Portsmouth, New Hampshire: Heinemann, 1983.

Propp, V. *Morphology of the Folktale*. Austin: University of Texas Press, 2001.

Pullman, P. *Imaginary Friends (from Daemon Voices)*. Oxford: David Fickling Books, 2017.

Roberts, C., Livingstone, H. & Baxter-Wright, E. *Goth: The Designs, Art and Fashion of a Dark Subculture*. London: Carlton Books, 2014.

Rockett, M. & Percival, S. *Thinking for Learning*. Stafford: Network Educational Press, 2002.

Rosenthal, R. *Pygmalion in the Classroom: Teacher Expectation and Pupils' Intellectual Development*. Bancyfelin, Carmarthen: Crown House Publishing, 2003.

Stock, G. *The Kids' Book of Questions*. New York: Workman Publishing Company, 2004.

Townshend, D. (Ed.). *Terror and Wonder: The Gothic Imagination*. London: The British Library, 2014.

Introduction

http://www.readingrockets.org/article/teaching-creative-writing.

https://www.jstor.org/stable/41405103 – Gail E. Thompkins and why children should be taught creative writing.

http://homes.lmc.gatech.edu/~mateas/nidocs/MateasSengers.pdf – narrative intelligence.

Fantasy story

http://bestfantasybooks.com/ – This is a useful website for listing subgenres of fantasy, with recommendations of books, movies and games.

Science fiction story

https://futurism.media/history-of-science-fiction-part-i – This is a useful website exploring the history and other aspects of science fiction in books, films and on TV.

https://www.learning-theories.com/cognitive-tools-theory-egan.html.

https://www.quora.com/How-did-certain-English-nouns-e-g-car-ship-country-earth-go-to-the-feminine-gender.

https://www.commonsensemedia.org/movie-reviews/the-war-of-the-worlds-1953/user-reviews/adult – re age rating.

Pirate story

http://www.piratemerch.com/pirate_name_generator.

Thriller story

https://www.storycubes.com/.

Gothic fiction

https://www.parent24.com/Child_7-12/Fun/Should-your-child-read-horror-stories-20151019.

https://www.barnesandnoble.com/blog/5-reasons-horror-in-childrens-literature-is-a-good-thing/.

https://www.theguardian.com/books/2016/aug/25/one-third-of-parents-avoid-reading-children-scary-stories-study-finds.

http://creepworld.com/2016/03/24/good-kids-read-scary-stories/.

https://www.tes.com/news/why-fairy-tales-are-horror-stories-we-need-be-more-wary-schools.

http://sciencenordic.com/why-horror-so-popular.

http://www.scottishbooktrust.com/blog/teachers-librarians/2017/12/5-tips-to-explore-gothic-fiction-with-children.

http://myths.e2bn.org/teachers/info311-what-are-myths-legends-and-folktales.html.

https://www.independent.co.uk/news/world/europe/the-truth-about-urban-myths-543013.html.

https://lisdemo.libguides.com/c.php?g=385569&p=2614106 – vampires in children's literature.

General tips when teaching writing

http://www3.canisius.edu/~justice/CSTmodule-final/CSTmodule-final18.html –
scaffolding students' work.

http://authenticlearning.weebly.com/.

http://www3.canisius.edu/~justice/CSTmodule-final/CSTmodule-final17.html –
the Process Approach.

https://files.eric.ed.gov/fulltext/EJ1082330.pdf – more on the Process Approach.

http://www.talk4writing.co.uk/portfolio-items/inventing-stories/ – imitate, innovate, invent.